SCARLET

Twenty-One Designs

By

Kim Hargreaves

CREDITS

DESIGNS & STYLING
Kim Hargreaves

EDITOR
Kathleen Hargreaves

MODEL
Naomi Vergette-D'Souza

HAIR & MAKE-UP
Diana Fisher

PHOTOGRAPHY & EDITORIAL DESIGN
Graham Watts

LAYOUTS
Angela Lin

PATTERNS
Sue Whiting & Trisha McKenzie

© Copyright Kim Hargreaves 2011
First published in 2011 by Kim Hargreaves, Intake Cottage, 26 Underbank Old Road, Holmfirth, West Yorkshire, HD9 1EA, England.

British Library Cataloguing in Publication Data
A catalogue record for this book is available from the British Library.

ISBN-10   1-906487-12-6
ISBN-13   978-1-906487-12-6

CONTENTS

THE
STORY

A carefree spirit sweeps through secluded forests
and engaging landscapes, in perfect harmony
with this season's relaxed textures and mellow tones.
Wrapped in layers of cosy cables, blanket like stripes,
and hazy arans for a blissful adventure into
natures heartland.

LOVE | A DELICATE CABLE & LACE CARDIGAN, WORN WITH A SNUG HAT | TRANCE

STEED | A FITTED JACKET
WORKED IN MOSS STITCH,
WITH CURVED HEMLINE &
BACK PEPLUM

10

HOMESPUN | THIS PAGE
COSY OPEN STITCH SCARF

WARRIOR | OPPOSITE
A COCOON LIKE SWEATER
WITH TRAVELLING CABLES

SHEARLING | A COSY SHAWL
COLLARED WAISTCOAT WITH
ASYMMETRIC FRONTS

15

BLAZE | A SEMI-FITTED
ARAN SWEATER WITH
A SOFT NECK-LINE

25

RUMOUR | A SOFT
V-NECKED CARDIGAN
WITH PRETTY HEMLINE
DETAILING

WHITTLE SNUG
MITTENS WORKED IN A
SHAPED RIBBING

HEARTLAND | A BOXY
CROCHET JACKET
WORKED IN A COSY,
CHUNKY FABRIC

35

THORN | A CLOSE-FITTING CARDIGAN WITH SQUARE NECK-LINE, WORKED IN AN EYELET PATTERN

HUNTER | A CROPPED BOXY SWEATER WITH EYELETS & CABLES

TRANCE | A CLOSE-FITTING
HAT WITH COSY RIBBING

MOONSTONE | THIS PAGE,
A DELICATE SHORT-FITTING
CARDIGAN.

LEAF | OPPOSITE,
A CLASSIC CARDIGAN
WITH SHAWL FRONTS
& CUFF DETAILS,

BRACKEN | A SNUG
LONG-LINE
FRINGED SCARF

THE
END

LOVE
Delicate lace & cable cardigan

Recommendation
Suitable for the knitter with a little experience
Please see pages 7, 8 & 9 for photographs.

	XS	S	M	L	XL	XXL	
To fit	**81**	**86**	**91**	**97**	**102**	**109**	**cm**
bust	32	34	36	38	40	43	in

Rowan Pima Cotton
| | 9 | 9 | 10 | 10 | 11 | 11 | x 50gm |

Photographed in Pampas

Needles
1 pair 2¾mm (no 12) (US 2) needles
1 pair 3¼mm (no 10) (US 3) needles
Cable needle

Buttons - 7

Tension
26 sts and 34 rows to 10 cm measured over
pattern using 3¼mm (US 3) needles.

Special abbreviations
C6B = slip next 3 sts onto cable needle and
leave at back of work, K3, then K3 from cable
needle.
C6F = slip next 3 sts onto cable needle and
leave at front of work, K3, then K3 from cable
needle.

BACK
Cast on 111 (117: 123: 129: 137: 147) sts
using 2¾mm (US 2) needles.
Row 1 (RS): K1 (0: 1: 0: 0: 1), *P1, K1, rep
from * to last 0 (1: 0: 1: 1: 0) st, P0 (1: 0: 1:
1: 0).
Row 2: P1 (0: 1: 0: 0: 1), *K1, P1, rep from
* to last 0 (1: 0: 1: 1: 0) st, K0 (1: 0: 1: 1: 0).
These 2 rows form rib.
Work in rib for a further 21 rows, ending with
a **RS** row.
Row 24 (WS): Rib 18 (21: 24: 25: 29: 34),
M1, rib 4, M1, rib 15 (15: 15: 17: 17: 17), M1,
rib 4, M1, rib 13, M1, rib 3, M1, rib 13, M1, rib
4, M1, rib 15 (15: 15: 17: 17: 17), M1, rib 4,
M1, rib 18 (21: 24: 25: 29: 34).
121 (127: 133: 139: 147: 157) sts.
Change to 3¼mm (US 3) needles.
Now work in patt as folls:
Row 1 (RS): P1 (0: 1: 0: 0: 1), (K1, P1) 7
(9: 10: 11: 13: 15) times, P1, K6, P1 (1: 1:
2: 2: 2), K3, K2tog, (yfwd, K1) 7 times, yfwd,
sl 1, K1, psso, K3, P1 (1: 1: 2: 2: 2), K6, P1,
P2tog, yrn, P6, K9, P6, yrn, P2tog tbl, P1,
K6, P1 (1: 1: 2: 2: 2), K3, K2tog, (yfwd, K1)
7 times, yfwd, sl 1, K1, psso, K3, P1 (1: 1: 2:
2: 2), K6, P1, (P1, K1) 7 (9: 10: 11: 13: 15)
times, P1 (0: 1: 0: 0: 1).
Row 2: K1 (0: 1: 0: 0: 1), (P1, K1) 7 (9: 10:
11: 13: 15) times, K1, P6, K1 (1: 1: 2: 2: 2),
P2, P1 and slip this st back onto left needle,
now lift 2nd st on left needle over this st
and off left needle and slip original st
back onto right needle, P15, P2tog, P2,
K1 (1: 1: 2: 2: 2), P6, K9, P9, K9, P6, K1
(1: 1: 2: 2: 2), P2, P1 and slip this st back
onto left needle, now lift 2nd st on left
needle over this st and off left needle
and slip original st back onto right needle,
P15, P2tog, P2, K1 (1: 1: 2: 2: 2), P6, K1,
(K1, P1) 7 (9: 10: 11: 13: 15) times, K1 (0:
1: 0: 0: 1).
Row 3: K1 (0: 1: 0: 0: 1), (P1, K1) 7 (9: 10:
11: 13: 15) times, P1, K6, P1 (1: 1: 2: 2: 2),
K1, K2tog, K15, sl 1, K1, psso, K1, P1 (1: 1:
2: 2), K6, P3, yrn, P2tog tbl, P4, K3, C6F, P4,
P2tog, yrn, P3, K6, P1 (1: 1: 2: 2: 2), K1, K2tog,
K15, sl 1, K1, psso, K1, P1 (1: 1: 2: 2: 2), K6,
P1, (K1, P1) 7 (9: 10: 11: 13: 15) times, K1 (0:
1: 0: 0: 1).

Row 4: P1 (0: 1: 0: 0: 1), (K1, P1) 7 (9: 10:
11: 13: 15) times, K1, P6, K1 (1: 1: 2: 2:
2), P1 and slip this st back onto left needle,
now lift 2nd st on left needle over this st
and off left needle and slip original st back
onto right needle, P15, P2tog, K1 (1: 1: 2:
2: 2), P6, K9, P9, K9, P6, K1 (1: 1: 2: 2: 2),
P1 and slip this st back onto left needle,
now lift 2nd st on left needle over this st
and off left needle and slip original st back
onto right needle, P15, P2tog, K1 (1: 1: 2:
2: 2), P6, K1, (P1, K1) 7 (9: 10: 11: 13: 15)
times, P1 (0: 1: 0: 0: 1).
These 4 rows form patt for edge 15 (18: 21:
22: 26: 31) sts and lace panels between
cables.
(**Note:** Number of sts varies whilst working lace
panels. All st counts given presume there are
17 sts in lace panels at all times.)
Keeping these sections correct as now set, cont
as folls:
Row 5: Patt 15 (18: 21: 22: 26: 31) sts, P1,
C6B, P1 (1: 1: 2: 2: 2), patt 17 sts, P1 (1: 1:
2: 2: 2), C6B, P4, yrn, P2tog tbl, P3, K9, P3,
P2tog, yrn, P4, C6F, P1 (1: 1: 2: 2: 2), patt 17
sts, P1 (1: 1: 2: 2: 2), C6F, P1, patt 15 (18: 21:
22: 26: 31) sts.
Row 6: Patt 15 (18: 21: 22: 26: 31) sts, K1,
P6, K1 (1: 1: 2: 2: 2), patt 17 sts, K1 (1: 1: 2:
2: 2), P6, K9, P9, K9, P6, K1 (1: 1: 2: 2: 2), patt
17 sts, K1 (1: 1: 2: 2: 2), P6, K1, patt 15 (18:
21: 22: 26: 31) sts.
Row 7: Patt 15 (18: 21: 22: 26: 31) sts, P1,
K6, P1 (1: 1: 2: 2: 2), patt 17 sts, P1 (1: 1: 2:
2: 2), K6, P5, yrn, P2tog tbl, P2, K9, P2, P2tog,
yrn, P5, K6, P1 (1: 1: 2: 2: 2), patt 17 sts, P1
(1: 1: 2: 2: 2), K6, P1, patt 15 (18: 21: 22: 26:
31) sts.
Row 8: Patt 15 (18: 21: 22: 26: 31) sts, K1,
P6, K1 (1: 1: 2: 2: 2), patt 17 sts, K1 (1: 1: 2:
2: 2), P6, K9, P9, K9, P6, K1 (1: 1: 2: 2: 2), patt
17 sts, K1 (1: 1: 2: 2: 2), P6, K1, patt 15 (18:
21: 22: 26: 31) sts.
These 8 rows form patt for cables either side
of lacy panels.
Keeping these sections correct as now set,
cont as folls:
Row 9: Patt 47 (50: 53: 56: 60: 65) sts, P6,
yrn, P2tog tbl, P1, C6B, K3, P1, P2tog, yrn, P6,
patt 47 (50: 53: 56: 60: 65) sts.

Row 10: Patt 47 (50: 53: 56: 60: 65) sts, K9, P9, K9, patt 47 (50: 53: 56: 60: 65) sts.
Row 11: Patt 47 (50: 53: 56: 60: 65) sts, P4, P2tog, yrn, P3, K9, P3, yrn, P2tog tbl, P4, patt 47 (50: 53: 56: 60: 65) sts.
Row 12: Patt 47 (50: 53: 56: 60: 65) sts, K9, P9, K9, patt 47 (50: 53: 56: 60: 65) sts.
These 12 rows form patt for centre cable.
Keeping this section correct as now set, cont as folls:
Row 13: Patt 47 (50: 53: 56: 60: 65) sts, P3, P2tog, yrn, P4, patt 9 sts, P4, yrn, P2tog tbl, P3, patt 47 (50: 53: 56: 60: 65) sts.
Row 14: Patt 47 (50: 53: 56: 60: 65) sts, K9, patt 9 sts, K9, patt 47 (50: 53: 56: 60: 65) sts.
Row 15: Patt 47 (50: 53: 56: 60: 65) sts, P2, P2tog, yrn, P5, patt 9 sts, P5, yrn, P2tog tbl, P2, patt 47 (50: 53: 56: 60: 65) sts.
Row 16: Patt 47 (50: 53: 56: 60: 65) sts, K9, patt 9 sts, K9, patt 47 (50: 53: 56: 60: 65) sts.
These 16 rows form patt for zig zag lace sections either side of centre cable.
Keeping all sections correct as now set, cont as folls:
Cont straight until back measures 27 (27: 28: 28: 28: 28) cm, ending with a WS row.
Shape armholes
Keeping patt correct, cast off 5 (5: 6: 6: 7: 7) sts at beg of next 2 rows.
111 (117: 121: 127: 133: 143) sts.
Dec 1 st at each end of next 5 (5: 7: 7: 9: 11) rows, then on foll 2 (4: 3: 4: 4: 5) alt rows, then on 2 foll 4th rows.
93 (95: 97: 101: 103: 107) sts.
Cont straight until armhole measures 18 (19: 19: 20: 21: 22) cm, ending with a WS row.
Shape shoulders and back neck
Cast off 9 (9: 9: 10: 10: 11) sts at beg of next 2 rows.
75 (77: 79: 81: 83: 85) sts.
Next row (RS): Cast off 9 (9: 9: 10: 10: 11) sts, patt until there are 13 (13: 14: 13: 14: 14) sts on right needle and turn, leaving rem sts on a holder.
Work each side of neck separately.
Cast off 4 sts at beg of next row.
Cast off rem 9 (9: 10: 9: 10: 10) sts.
With RS facing, rejoin yarn to rem sts, cast off centre 31 (33: 33: 35: 35: 35) sts, patt to end.
Complete to match first side, reversing shapings.

Pattern note: Row-end edges of fronts forms actual front opening edges. To ensure edges remains neat and tidy, make sure new balls of yarn are joined in at side seam edges **only**.

LEFT FRONT

Cast on 64 (67: 70: 73: 77: 82) sts using 2¾mm (US 2) needles.
Row 1 (RS): P0 (1: 0: 1: 1: 0), *K1, P1, rep from * to last 12 sts, K2, P2, (K1, P1) 4 times.
Row 2: (K1, P1) 4 times, K2, P2, *K1, P1, rep from * to last 0 (1: 0: 1: 1: 0) st, K0 (1: 0: 1: 1: 0).
Row 3: P0 (1: 0: 1: 1: 0), *K1, P1, rep from * to last 12 sts, K2, (P1, K1) 5 times.
Row 4: (P1, K1) 5 times, P2, *K1, P1, rep from * to last 0 (1: 0: 1: 1: 0) st, K0 (1: 0: 1: 1: 0).
These 4 rows form patt.
Work in patt for a further 19 rows, ending with a RS row.
Row 24 (WS): Patt 23 sts, M1, rib 4, M1, rib 15 (15: 15: 17: 17: 17), M1, rib 4, M1, rib 18 (21: 24: 25: 29: 34).
68 (71: 74: 77: 81: 86) sts.
Change to 3¼mm (US 3) needles.
Now work in patt as folls:
Row 1 (RS): P1 (0: 1: 0: 0: 1), (K1, P1) 7 (9: 10: 11: 13: 15) times, P1, K6, P1 (1: 1: 2: 2: 2), K3, K2tog, (yfwd, K1) 7 times, yfwd, sl 1, K1, psso, K3, P1 (1: 1: 2: 2: 2), K6, P1, P2tog, yrn, P6, patt 12 sts.
Row 2: Patt 12 sts, K9, P6, K1 (1: 1: 2: 2: 2), P2, P1 and slip this st back onto left needle, now lift 2nd st on left needle over this st and off left needle and slip original st back onto right needle, P15, P2tog, P2, K1 (1: 1: 2: 2: 2), P6, K1, (K1, P1) 7 (9: 10: 11: 13: 15) times, K1 (0: 1: 0: 0: 1).
Row 3: K1 (0: 1: 0: 0: 1), (P1, K1) 7 (9: 10: 11: 13: 15) times, P1, K6, P1 (1: 1: 2: 2: 2), K1, K2tog, K15, sl 1, K1, psso, K1, P1 (1: 1: 2: 2: 2), K6, P3, yrn, P2tog tbl, P4, patt 12 sts.
Row 4: Patt 12 sts, K9, P6, K1 (1: 1: 2: 2: 2), P1 and slip this st back onto left needle, now lift 2nd st on left needle over this st and off left needle and slip original st back onto right needle, P15, P2tog, K1 (1: 1: 2: 2: 2), P6, K1, (P1, K1) 7 (9: 10: 11: 13: 15) times, P1 (0: 1: 0: 0: 1).
These 4 rows form patt for edge 15 (18: 21: 22: 26: 31) sts and lace panel between cable.
(**Note:** Number of sts varies whilst working lace panel. All st counts given presume there are 17 sts in lace panel at all times.)
Keeping these sections correct as now set, cont as folls:
Row 5: Patt 15 (18: 21: 22: 26: 31) sts, P1, C6B, P1 (1: 1: 2: 2: 2), patt 17 sts, P1 (1: 1: 2: 2: 2), C6B, P4, yrn, P2tog tbl, P3, patt 12 sts.
Row 6: Patt 12 sts, K9, P6, K1 (1: 1: 2: 2: 2), patt 17 sts, K1 (1: 1: 2: 2: 2), P6, K1, patt 15 (18: 21: 22: 26: 31) sts.

Row 7: Patt 15 (18: 21: 22: 26: 31) sts, P1, K6, P1 (1: 1: 2: 2: 2), patt 17 sts, P1 (1: 1: 2: 2: 2), K6, P5, yrn, P2tog tbl, P2, patt 12 sts.
Row 8: Patt 12 sts, K9, P6, K1 (1: 1: 2: 2: 2), patt 17 sts, K1 (1: 1: 2: 2: 2), P6, K1, patt 15 (18: 21: 22: 26: 31) sts.
These 8 rows form patt for cables either side of lacy panels.
Keeping these sections correct as now set, cont as folls:
Row 9: Patt 47 (50: 53: 56: 60: 65) sts, P6, yrn, P2tog tbl, P1, patt 12 sts.
Row 10: Patt 12 sts, K9, patt 47 (50: 53: 56: 60: 65) sts.
Row 11: Patt 47 (50: 53: 56: 60: 65) sts, P4, P2tog, yrn, P3, patt 12 sts.
Row 12: Patt 12 sts, K9, patt 47 (50: 53: 56: 60: 65) sts.
Row 13: Patt 47 (50: 53: 56: 60: 65) sts, P3, P2tog, yrn, P4, patt 12 sts.
Row 14: Patt 12 sts, K9, patt 47 (50: 53: 56: 60: 65) sts.
Row 15: Patt 47 (50: 53: 56: 60: 65) sts, P2, P2tog, yrn, P5, patt 12 sts.
Row 16: Patt 12 sts, K9, patt 47 (50: 53: 56: 60: 65) sts.
These 16 rows form patt for zig zag lace section near front opening edge.
Keeping all sections correct as now set, cont as folls:
Cont straight until left front matches back to start of armhole shaping, ending with a WS row.
Shape armhole
Keeping patt correct, cast off 5 (5: 6: 6: 7: 7) sts at beg of next row.
63 (66: 68: 71: 74: 79) sts.
Work 1 row.
Dec 1 st at armhole edge of next 5 (5: 7: 7: 9: 11) rows, then on foll 2 (4: 3: 4: 4: 5) alt rows, then on 2 foll 4th rows.
54 (55: 56: 58: 59: 61) sts.
Cont straight until 22 (22: 22: 26: 26: 26) rows less have been worked than on back to start of shoulder shaping, ending with a WS row.
Shape front neck
Next row (RS): Patt 39 (39: 40: 42: 43: 45) sts and turn, leaving rem 15 (16: 16: 16: 16: 16) sts on a holder.
Keeping patt correct, dec 1 st at neck edge of next 8 rows, then on foll 3 alt rows, then on 1 (1: 1: 2: 2: 2) foll 4th rows.
27 (27: 28: 29: 30: 32) sts.
Work 3 rows, ending with a WS row.

Shape shoulder

Cast off 9 (9: 9: 10: 10: 11) sts at beg of next and foll alt row.

Work 1 row.

Cast off rem 9 (9: 10: 9: 10: 10) sts.

Mark positions for 7 buttons along left front opening edge - first to come level with row 5, last to come level with first row of neck shaping, and rem 5 buttons evenly spaced between.

RIGHT FRONT

Cast on 64 (67: 70: 73: 77: 82) sts using 2¾mm (US 2) needles.

Row 1 (RS): (P1, K1) 4 times, P2, K2, *P1, K1, rep from * to last 0 (1: 0: 1: 1: 0) st, P0 (1: 0: 1: 1: 0).

Row 2: K0 (1: 0: 1: 1: 0), *P1, K1, rep from * to last 12 sts, P2, K2, (P1, K1) 4 times.

Row 3: (K1, P1) 5 times, K2, *P1, K1, rep from * to last 0 (1: 0: 1: 1: 0) st, P0 (1: 0: 1: 1: 0).

Row 4: K0 (1: 0: 1: 1: 0), *P1, K1, rep from * to last 12 sts, P2, (K1, P1) 5 times.

These 4 rows form patt.

Row 5 (RS): Patt 2 sts, work 2 tog, yrn (to make a buttonhole), patt to end.

Working a further 6 buttonholes in this way to correspond with positions marked for buttons on left front and noting that no further reference will be made to buttonholes, cont as folls:

Work in patt for a further 18 rows, ending with a **RS** row.

Row 24 (WS): Rib 18 (21: 24: 25: 29: 34), M1, rib 4, M1, rib 15 (15: 15: 17: 17: 17), M1, rib 4, M1, patt 23 sts. 68 (71: 74: 77: 81: 86) sts.

Change to 3¼mm (US 3) needles.

Now work in patt as folls:

Row 1 (RS): Patt 12 sts, P6, yrn, P2tog tbl, P1, K6, P1 (1: 1: 2: 2: 2), K3, K2tog, (yfwd, K1) 7 times, yfwd, sl 1, K1, psso, K3, P1 (1: 1: 2: 2: 2), K6, P1, (P1, K1) 7 (9: 10: 11: 13: 15) times, P1 (0: 1: 0: 0: 1).

Row 2: K1 (0: 1: 0: 0: 1), (P1, K1) 7 (9: 10: 11: 13: 15) times, K1, P6, K1 (1: 1: 2: 2: 2), P2, P1 and slip this st back onto left needle, now lift 2nd st on left needle over this st and off left needle and slip original st back onto right needle, P15, P2tog, P2, K1 (1: 1: 2: 2: 2), P6, K9, patt 12 sts.

Row 3: Patt 12 sts, P4, P2tog, yrn, P3, K6, P1 (1: 1: 2: 2: 2), K1, K2tog, K15, sl 1, K1, psso, K1, P1 (1: 1: 2: 2: 2), K6, P1, (K1, P1) 7 (9: 10: 11: 13: 15) times, K1 (0: 1: 0: 0: 1).

Row 4: P1 (0: 1: 0: 0: 1), (K1, P1) 7 (9: 10: 11: 13: 15) times, K1, P6, K1 (1: 1: 2: 2: 2),

P1 and slip this st back onto left needle, now lift 2nd st on left needle over this st and off left needle and slip original st back onto right needle, P15, P2tog, K1 (1: 1: 2: 2: 2), P6, K9, patt 12 sts.

These 4 rows form patt for edge 15 (18: 21: 22: 26: 31) sts and lace panel between cable.

(**Note:** Number of sts varies whilst working lace panel. All st counts given presume there are 17 sts in lace panel at all times.)

Keeping these sections correct as now set, cont as folls:

Row 5: Patt 12 sts, P3, P2tog, yrn, P4, C6F, P1 (1: 1: 2: 2: 2), patt 17 sts, P1 (1: 1: 2: 2: 2), C6F, P1, patt 15 (18: 21: 22: 26: 31) sts.

Row 6: Patt 15 (18: 21: 22: 26: 31) sts, K1, P6, K1 (1: 1: 2: 2: 2), patt 17 sts, K1 (1: 1: 2: 2: 2), P6, K9, patt 12 sts.

Row 7: Patt 12 sts, P2, P2tog, yrn, P5, K6, P1 (1: 1: 2: 2: 2), patt 17 sts, P1 (1: 1: 2: 2: 2), K6, P1, patt 15 (18: 21: 22: 26: 31) sts.

Row 8: Patt 15 (18: 21: 22: 26: 31) sts, K1, P6, K1 (1: 1: 2: 2: 2), patt 17 sts, K1 (1: 1: 2: 2: 2), P6, K9, patt 12 sts.

These 8 rows form patt for cables either side of lacy panels.

Keeping these sections correct as now set, cont as folls:

Row 9: Patt 12 sts, P1, P2tog, yrn, P6, patt 47 (50: 53: 56: 60: 65) sts.

Row 10: Patt 47 (50: 53: 56: 60: 65) sts, K9, patt 12 sts.

Row 11: Patt 12 sts, P3, yrn, P2tog tbl, P4, patt 47 (50: 53: 56: 60: 65) sts.

Row 12: Patt 47 (50: 53: 56: 60: 65) sts, K9, patt 12 sts.

Row 13: Patt 12 sts, P4, yrn, P2tog tbl, P3, patt 47 (50: 53: 56: 60: 65) sts.

Row 14: Patt 47 (50: 53: 56: 60: 65) sts, K9, patt 12 sts.

Row 15: Patt 12 sts, P5, yrn, P2tog tbl, P2, patt 47 (50: 53: 56: 60: 65) sts.

Row 16: Patt 47 (50: 53: 56: 60: 65) sts, K9, patt 12 sts.

These 16 rows form patt for zig zag lace section near front opening edge.

Keeping all sections correct as now set, complete to match left front, reversing shapings and working first row of neck shaping as folls:

Shape front neck

Next row (RS): Patt 2 sts, work 2 tog, yrn (to make 7th buttonhole), patt 11 (12: 12: 12: 12: 12) sts and slip these 15 (16: 16: 16: 16: 16) sts onto a holder, patt to end.

39 (39: 40: 42: 43: 45) sts.

SLEEVES (both alike)

Cast on 65 (67: 69: 71: 75: 77) sts using 2¾mm (US 2) needles.

Row 1 (RS): K1, *P1, K1, rep from * to end.

Row 2: P1, *K1, P1, rep from * to end.

These 2 rows form rib.

Work in rib for a further 21 rows, inc 1 st at each end of 15th of these rows and ending with a **RS** row. 67 (69: 71: 73: 77: 79) sts.

Row 24 (WS): Rib 22 (23: 24: 24: 26: 27), M1, rib 4, M1, rib 15 (15: 15: 17: 17: 17), M1, rib 4, M1, rib 22 (23: 24: 24: 26: 27). 71 (73: 75: 77: 81: 83) sts.

Change to 3¼mm (US 3) needles.

Now work in patt as folls:

Row 1 (RS): P1 (0: 1: 1: 1: 0), (K1, P1) 9 (10: 10: 10: 11: 12) times, P1, K6, P1 (1: 1: 2: 2: 2), K3, K2tog, (yfwd, K1) 7 times, yfwd, sl 1, K1, psso, K3, P1 (1: 1: 2: 2: 2), K6, P1, (P1, K1) 9 (10: 10: 10: 11: 12) times, P1 (0: 1: 1: 1: 0).

Row 2: K1 (0: 1: 1: 1: 0), (P1, K1) 9 (10: 10: 10: 11: 12) times, K1, P6, K1 (1: 1: 2: 2: 2), P2, P1 and slip this st back onto left needle, now lift 2nd st on left needle over this st and off left needle and slip original st back onto right needle, P15, P2tog, P2, K1 (1: 1: 2: 2: 2), P6, K1, (K1, P1) 9 (10: 10: 10: 11: 12) times, K1 (0: 1: 1: 1: 0).

Row 3: K1 (0: 1: 1: 1: 0), (P1, K1) 9 (10: 10: 10: 11: 12) times, P1, K6, P1 (1: 1: 2: 2: 2), K1, K2tog, K15, sl 1, K1, psso, K1, P1 (1: 1: 2: 2: 2), K6, P1, (K1, P1) 9 (10: 10: 10: 11: 12) times, K1 (0: 1: 1: 1: 0).

Row 4: P1 (0: 1: 1: 1: 0), (K1, P1) 9 (10: 10: 10: 11: 12) times, K1, P6, K1 (1: 1: 2: 2: 2), P1 and slip this st back onto left needle, now lift 2nd st on left needle over this st and off left needle and slip original st back onto right needle, P15, P2tog, K1 (1: 1: 2: 2: 2), P6, K1, (P1, K1) 9 (10: 10: 10: 11: 12) times, P1 (0: 1: 1: 1: 0).

These 4 rows form patt for edge 19 (20: 21: 21: 23: 24) sts and lace panel at centre.

(**Note:** Number of sts varies whilst working lace panel. All st counts given presume there are 17 sts in lace panel at all times.)

Keeping these sections correct as now set, cont as folls:

Row 5: Patt 19 (20: 21: 21: 23: 24) sts, P1, C6F, P1 (1: 1: 2: 2: 2), patt 17 sts, P1 (1: 1: 2: 2: 2), C6B, P1, patt 19 (20: 21: 21: 23: 24) sts.

Row 6: Patt 19 (20: 21: 21: 23: 24) sts, K1, P6, K1 (1: 1: 2: 2: 2), patt 17 sts, K1 (1: 1: 2: 2: 2), P6, K1, patt 19 (20: 21: 21: 23: 24) sts.

Row 7: Patt 19 (20: 21: 21: 23: 24) sts, P1, K6, P1 (1: 1: 2: 2: 2), patt 17 sts, P1 (1: 1: 2: 2: 2), K6, P1, patt 19 (20: 21: 21: 23: 24) sts.

Row 8: Patt 19 (20: 21: 21: 23: 24) sts, K1, P6, K1, P6, K1 (1: 1: 2: 2: 2), patt 17 sts, K1 (1: 1: 2: 2: 2), P6, K1, patt 19 (20: 21: 21: 23: 24) sts.
These 8 rows form patt for cables either side of lacy panel.
Keeping these sections correct as now set, cont as folls:
Inc 1 st at each end of next and 1 (1: 1: 3: 5: 5) foll 16th rows, then on 4 (4: 4: 2: 0: 0) foll 14th rows, taking inc sts into double moss st.
83 (85: 87: 89: 93: 95) sts.
Cont straight until sleeve measures 33 (34: 35: 36: 37: 38) cm, ending with a WS row.

Shape top
Keeping patt correct, cast off 5 (5: 6: 6: 7: 7) sts at beg of next 2 rows.
73 (75: 75: 77: 79: 81) sts.
Dec 1 st at each end of next 3 rows, then on foll alt row, then on 7 foll 4th rows.
51 (53: 53: 55: 57: 59) sts.
Work 1 row.
Dec 1 st at each end of next and every foll alt row to 45 sts, then on foll 5 rows, ending with a WS row.
Cast off rem 35 sts.

MAKING UP
Press all pieces with a warm iron over a damp cloth.
Join both shoulder seams using back stitch or mattress stitch if preferred.
(**Note**: The top cast-off edge of the lacy panel will form a definite curve that would distort the shoulder seams. Take some of this extra fabric into seam when sewing shoulders so that seam is straight.)

Neckband
With RS facing and using 2¾mm (US 2) needles, slip 15 (16: 16: 16: 16: 16) sts on right front holder onto right needle, rejoin yarn and pick up and knit 20 (20: 20: 24: 24: 24) sts up right side of neck, 29 (31: 31: 33: 33: 33) sts from back, and 20 (20: 20: 24: 24: 24) sts down left side of neck, then patt 15 (16: 16: 16: 16: 16) sts on left front holder.
99 (103: 103: 113: 113: 113) sts.
Row 1 (WS): Patt 12 sts, K1, *P1, K1, rep from * to last 12 sts, patt 12 sts.
Row 2: Patt 12 sts, P1, *K1, P1, rep from * to last 12 sts, patt 12 sts.
These 2 rows set the sts - 12 sts at each end of rows still in patt with all other sts in rib.
Cont as set for a further 4 rows, ending with a RS row.
Cast off in patt (on WS).
Join side seams. Join sleeve seams. Insert sleeves into armholes. Sew on buttons.

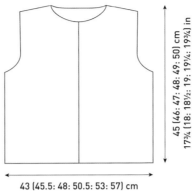

45 (46: 47: 48: 49: 50) cm
17¾ (18: 18½: 19: 19¼: 19¾) in

43 (45.5: 48: 50.5: 53: 57) cm
17 (18: 19: 20: 21: 22½) in

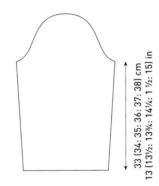

33 (34: 35: 36: 37: 38) cm
13 (13½: 13¾: 14¼: 1 ½: 15) in

STEED
Sculptured peplum jacket

Recommendation

Suitable for the knitter with a little experience
Please see pages 10 & 11 for photographs.

	XS	S	M	L	XL	XXL	
To fit	**81**	**86**	**91**	**97**	**102**	**109**	cm
bust	32	34	36	38	40	43	in

Rowan Felted Tweed Aran

| | 11 | 12 | 12 | 13 | 14 | 15 | x 50gm |

Photographed in Dusty

Needles

1 pair 3¾mm (no 9) (US 5) needles
1 pair 4½mm (no 7) (US 7) needles

Buttons - 19

Tension

17 sts and 29 rows to 10 cm measured over
moss st using 4½mm (US 7) needles.

BACK

Cast on 103 (107: 111: 115: 119: 127) sts
using 4½mm (US 7) needles.
Row 1 (RS): P1, (K1, P1) 6 (7: 8: 8: 9: 11)
times, P12, (K1, P1) 3 times, P12, (K1, P1)
9 (9: 9: 11: 11: 11) times, wrap next st (by
slipping next st from left needle onto right
needle, taking yarn to opposite side of work
between needles and then slipping same st
back onto left needle - when working back
across wrapped sts work the wrapped st and
the wrapping loop tog as one st) and turn.
Row 2: P1, (K1, P1) 9 (9: 9: 11: 11: 11) times,
wrap next st and turn.
Row 3: P1, (K1, P1) 9 (9: 9: 11: 11: 11) times,
P12, (K1, P1) 3 times, wrap next st and turn.
Row 4: P1, (K1, P1) 3 times, K11, P1, (K1, P1)
9 (9: 9: 11: 11: 11) times, K11, P1, (K1, P1)
3 times, wrap next st and turn.
Row 5: P1, (K1, P1) 3 times, P12, (K1, P1) 9
(9: 9: 11: 11: 11) times, P12, (K1, P1) 3 times,
P12, (K1, P1) twice, wrap next st and turn.
Row 6: P1, (K1, P1) twice, K11, P1, (K1, P1)
3 times, K11, P1, (K1, P1) 9 (9: 9: 11: 11: 11)
times, K11, P1, (K1, P1) 3 times, K11, P1, (K1,
P1) twice, wrap next st and turn.
Row 7: P1, (K1, P1) twice, P12, (K1, P1) 3
times, P12, (K1, P1) 9 (9: 9: 11: 11: 11) times,
P12, (K1, P1) 3 times, P12, (K1, P1) 4 (5: 5: 5:
6: 7) times, wrap next st and turn.
Row 8: P1, (K1, P1) 4 (5: 5: 5: 6: 7) times,
K11, P1, (K1, P1) 3 times, K11, P1, (K1, P1)
9 (9: 9: 11: 11: 11) times, K11, P1, (K1, P1)
3 times, K11, P1, (K1, P1) 4 (5: 5: 5: 6: 7)
times, wrap next st and turn.
Row 9: P1, (K1, P1) 4 (5: 5: 5: 6: 7) times,
P12, (K1, P1) 3 times, P12, (K1, P1) 9 (9: 9:
11: 11: 11) times, P12, (K1, P1) 3 times, P12,
(K1, P1) 6 (7: 8: 8: 9: 11) times.
Row 10: P1, (K1, P1) 6 (7: 8: 8: 9: 11) times,
*place marker on needle, K11, place marker
on needle*, P1, (K1, P1) 3 times, rep from * to
* once more, P1, (K1, P1) 9 (9: 9: 11: 11: 11)
times, rep from * to * once more, P1, (K1, P1)
3 times, rep from * to * once more, P1, (K1, P1)
6 (7: 8: 8: 9: 11) times. (8 markers in total.)
These 10 rows set the sts - 4 panels of rev st st
between markers with all other sts in moss st.
Keeping sts correct as now set, cont as folls:
Work 8 rows, ending with a WS row.

Row 19 (RS): Work 2 tog, *moss st to marker,
slip marker onto right needle, P2tog, P to
within 2 sts of next marker, P2tog tbl, slip
marker onto right needle, rep from * 3 times
more, moss st to last 2 sts, work 2 tog.
93 (97: 101: 105: 109: 117) sts.
Work 9 rows.
Row 29: As row 19.
83 (87: 91: 95: 99: 107) sts.
Work 7 rows.
Row 37: As row 19.
73 (77: 81: 85: 89: 97) sts.
Work 5 rows.
Row 43: *Moss st to marker, slip marker
onto right needle, P2tog, P to within 2 sts
of next marker, P2tog tbl, slip marker onto
right needle, rep from * 3 times more, moss
st to end.
65 (69: 73: 77: 81: 89) sts.
Work 1 row.
Row 45: Work 2 tog, *moss st to marker,
slip marker onto right needle, P3tog, slip
marker onto right needle, rep from * 3 times
more, moss st to last 2 sts, work 2 tog.
55 (59: 63: 67: 71: 79) sts.
Remove markers.
Now working all sts in moss st, cont as folls:
Work 7 rows, ending with a WS row.
Place markers at both ends of last row
- these markers denote waist position.
Work 8 rows, ending with a WS row.
Inc 1 st at each end of next and 7 foll
6th rows, taking inc sts into moss st.
71 (75: 79: 83: 87: 95) sts.
Cont straight until back measures 21 (21: 22:
22: 22: 22) cm **from waist markers**, ending
with a WS row.
Shape armholes
Keeping moss st correct, cast off 3 sts at beg
of next 2 rows.
65 (69: 73: 77: 81: 89) sts.
Dec 1 st at each end of next 1 (3: 3: 5: 5: 7)
rows, then on foll 2 (1: 2: 1: 2: 3) alt rows,
then on foll 4th row.
57 (59: 61: 63: 65: 67) sts.
Cont straight until armhole measures 18 (19:
19: 20: 21: 22) cm, ending with a WS row.
Shape shoulders and back neck
Cast off 6 (6: 6: 6: 6: 7) sts at beg of next
2 rows. 45 (47: 49: 51: 53: 53) sts.

Next row (RS): Cast off 6 (6: 6: 6: 6: 7) sts, moss st until there are 9 (9: 10: 10: 11: 10) sts on right needle and turn, leaving rem sts on a holder.
Work each side of neck separately.
Cast off 4 sts at beg of next row.
Cast off rem 5 (5: 6: 6: 7: 6) sts.
With RS facing, rejoin yarn to rem sts, cast off centre 15 (17: 17: 19: 19: 19) sts, moss st to end.
Complete to match first side, reversing shapings.

Pattern note: Row-end edges of fronts forms actual front opening edges. To ensure edges remains neat and tidy, make sure new balls of yarn are joined in at side seam edges **only**.

LEFT FRONT
Cast on 43 (45: 47: 49: 51: 55) sts using 4½mm (US 7) needles.
Row 1 (RS): P1, (K1, P1) 1 (2: 3: 3: 4: 5) times, wrap next st and turn.
Row 2: P1, (K1, P1) 1 (2: 3: 3: 4: 5) times.
These 2 rows set position of moss st.
Keeping moss st correct and working extra sts in moss st, cont as folls:
Row 3: Moss st 11 (13: 15: 17: 19: 23) sts, wrap next st and turn.
Row 4: Moss st to end.
Row 5: Moss st 19 (21: 23: 25: 27: 31) sts, wrap next st and turn.
Row 6: Moss st to end.
Row 7: Moss st 25 (27: 29: 31: 33: 37) sts, wrap next st and turn.
Row 8: Moss st to end.
Row 9: Moss st 29 (31: 33: 35: 37: 41) sts, wrap next st and turn.
Row 10: Moss st to end.
Row 11: Work 2 tog, moss st 31 (33: 35: 37: 39: 43) sts, wrap next st and turn.
Row 12: Moss st to end.
Row 13: Moss st 36 (38: 40: 42: 44: 48) sts, wrap next st and turn.
Row 14: Moss st to end.
Row 15: Moss st 40 (42: 44: 46: 48: 52) sts, wrap next st and turn.
Row 16: Moss st to end.
Now working in moss st across all sts, cont as folls:
Work 4 rows, ending with a WS row.
Counting in from end of last row, place marker after 15th (15th: 15th: 17th: 17th: 17th) st.
Row 21: Work 2 tog, moss st to marker, slip marker onto right needle, work 3 tog, moss st to end. 39 (41: 43: 45: 47: 51) sts.
Work 7 rows.

Row 29: As row 21.
36 (38: 40: 42: 44: 48) sts.
Rep last 8 rows once more.
33 (35: 37: 39: 41: 45) sts.
Work 7 rows.
Place marker at end of last row - this marker denotes waist position.
Work 8 rows, ending with a WS row.
Inc 1 st at beg of next and 7 foll 6th rows, taking inc sts into moss st.
41 (43: 45: 47: 49: 53) sts.
Cont straight until left front matches back to start of armhole shaping, **matching lengths from waist markers** and ending with a WS row.
Shape armhole
Keeping moss st correct, cast off 3 sts at beg of next row.
38 (40: 42: 44: 46: 50) sts.
Work 1 row.
Dec 1 st at armhole edge of next 1 (3: 3: 5: 5: 7) rows, then on foll 2 (1: 2: 1: 2: 3) alt rows, then on foll 4th row.
34 (35: 36: 37: 38: 39) sts.
Cont straight until 12 (12: 12: 14: 14: 14) rows less have been worked than on back to start of shoulder shaping, ending with a WS row.
Shape front neck
Next row (RS): Moss st 26 (26: 27: 28: 29: 30) sts and turn, leaving rem 8 (9: 9: 9: 9: 9) sts on a holder.
Dec 1 st at neck edge of next 6 rows, then on foll 2 (2: 2: 3: 3: 3) alt rows. 18 (18: 19: 19: 20: 21) sts.
Work 1 row, ending with a WS row.
Shape shoulder
Cast off 6 (6: 6: 6: 6: 7) sts at beg of next and foll alt row and at same time dec 1 st at neck edge of next row.
Work 1 row.
Cast off rem 5 (5: 6: 6: 7: 6) sts.
Mark positions for 9 buttons along left front opening edge - first to come in first row after placement of waist marker, last to come 2.5 cm down from neck shaping, and rem 7 buttons evenly spaced between.

RIGHT FRONT
Cast on 43 (45: 47: 49: 51: 55) sts using 4½mm (US 7) needles.
Row 1 (RS): P1, *K1, P1, rep from * to end.
Row 2: P1, (K1, P1) 1 (2: 3: 3: 4: 5) times, wrap next st and turn.
These 2 rows set position of moss st.
Keeping moss st correct and working extra sts in moss st, cont as folls:

Row 3: Moss st to end.
Row 4: Moss st 11 (13: 15: 17: 19: 23) sts, wrap next st and turn.
Row 5: Moss st to end.
Row 6: Moss st 19 (21: 23: 25: 27: 31) sts, wrap next st and turn.
Row 7: Moss st to end.
Row 8: Moss st 25 (27: 29: 31: 33: 37) sts, wrap next st and turn.
Row 9: Moss st to end.
Row 10: Moss st 29 (31: 33: 35: 37: 41) sts, wrap next st and turn.
Row 11: Moss st to last 2 sts, work 2 tog.
Row 12: Moss st 32 (34: 36: 38: 40: 44) sts, wrap next st and turn.
Row 13: Moss st to end.
Row 14: Moss st 36 (38: 40: 42: 44: 48) sts, wrap next st and turn.
Row 15: **Moss st to end.**
Row 16: Moss st 40 (42: 44: 46: 48: 52) sts, wrap next st and turn.
Row 17: Moss st to end.
Now working in moss st across all sts, cont as folls:
Work 3 rows, ending with a WS row.
Counting in from beg of last row, place marker after 15th (15th: 15th: 17th: 17th: 17th) st.
Row 21: Moss st to within 3 sts of marker, work 3 tog tbl, slip marker onto right needle, moss st to last 2 sts, work 2 tog.
39 (41: 43: 45: 47: 51) sts.
Work 7 rows.
Row 29: As row 21.
36 (38: 40: 42: 44: 48) sts.
Rep last 8 rows once more.
33 (35: 37: 39: 41: 45) sts.
Work 7 rows.
Place marker at beg of last row - this marker denotes waist position.
Next row (RS): P1, K1, P2tog tbl, yrn (to make a buttonhole), moss st to end.
Working a further 8 buttonholes in this way to correspond with positions marked on left front for buttons and noting that no further reference will be made to buttonholes, cont as folls:
Work 7 rows, ending with a WS row.
Inc 1 st at end of next and 7 foll 6th rows, taking inc sts into moss st.
41 (43: 45: 47: 49: 53) sts.
Complete to match left front, reversing shapings and working first row of front neck shaping as folls:
Shape front neck
Next row (RS): Moss st 8 (9: 9: 9: 9: 9) sts and slip these sts onto a holder, moss st to end. 26 (26: 27: 28: 29: 30) sts.

RIGHT SLEEVE
Back cuff section
Cast on 13 (13: 15: 15: 17: 17) sts using 3¾mm (US 5) needles.
Work in g st for 3 rows, ending with a **RS** row.
Row 4 (WS): K1, *P1, K1, rep from * to end.
This row sets position of moss st.
Change to 4½mm (US 7) needles.
Cont in moss st, inc 1 st at end of 5th (7th: 7th: 9th: 9th: 7th) and foll 12th (12th: 14th: 14th: 14th: 12th) row. 15 (15: 17: 17: 19: 19) sts.
Work 11 (9: 7: 5: 5: 9) rows, ending with a WS row.
Break yarn and leave sts on a holder.

Front cuff section
Cast on 25 (27: 27: 29: 29: 29) sts using 3¾mm (US 5) needles.
Work in g st for 3 rows, ending with a **RS** row.
Row 4 (WS): K1, *P1, K1, rep from * to end.
This row sets position of moss st.
Change to 4½mm (US 7) needles.
Cont in moss st, inc 1 st at beg of 5th (7th: 7th: 9th: 9th: 7th) and foll 12th (12th: 14th: 14th: 14th: 12th) row. 27 (29: 29: 31: 31: 31) sts.
Work 11 (9: 7: 5: 5: 9) rows, ending with a WS row.

Join sections
Next row (RS): (Inc in first st) 1 (0: 0: 0: 0: 0) times, moss st to last 5 sts of front cuff section, holding RS of back cuff section against WS of front cuff section, P tog next st of front section with first st of back section, *K tog next st of front section with next st of back section, P tog next st of front section with next st of back section, rep from * once more, then moss st to last 1 (0: 0: 0: 0: 0) st of back cuff section, (inc in last st) 1 (0: 0: 0: 0: 0) times.
39 (39: 41: 43: 45: 45) sts.
**Cont in moss st across all sts and shape sides by inc 1 st at each end of 12th (2nd: 6th: 8th: 8th: 2nd) and every foll 12th (12th: 14th: 14th: 14th: 14th) row to 53 (53: 55: 55: 55: 61) sts, then on every foll - (14th: -: 16th: 16th: -) row until there are - (55: -: 57: 59: -) sts, taking inc sts into moss st.
Cont straight until sleeve measures 46 (47: 48: 49: 50: 51) cm, ending with a WS row.

Shape top
Keeping moss st correct, cast off 3 sts at beg of next 2 rows. 47 (49: 49: 51: 53: 55) sts.
Dec 1 st at each end of next and foll alt row, then on foll 4th row, then on 2 foll 6th rows, then on 2 foll 4th rows. 33 (35: 35: 37: 39: 41) sts.
Work 1 row.
Dec 1 st at each end of next and every foll alt row to 29 sts, then on foll 5 rows.
Cast off rem 19 sts.

LEFT SLEEVE
Front cuff section
Cast on 25 (27: 27: 29: 29: 29) sts using 3¾mm (US 5) needles.
Work in g st for 3 rows, ending with a **RS** row.
Row 4 (WS): K1, *P1, K1, rep from * to end.
This row sets position of moss st.
Change to 4½mm (US 7) needles.
Cont in moss st, inc 1 st at end of 5th (7th: 7th: 9th: 9th: 7th) and foll 12th (12th: 14th: 14th: 14th: 12th) row.
27 (29: 29: 31: 31: 31) sts.
Work 11 (9: 7: 5: 5: 9) rows, ending with a WS row.
Break yarn and leave sts on a holder.

Back cuff section
Cast on 13 (13: 15: 15: 17: 17) sts using 3¾mm (US 5) needles.
Work in g st for 3 rows, ending with a **RS** row.
Row 4 (WS): K1, *P1, K1, rep from * to end.
This row sets position of moss st.
Change to 4½mm (US 7) needles.
Cont in moss st, inc 1 st at beg of 5th (7th: 7th: 9th: 9th: 7th) and foll 12th (12th: 14th: 14th: 14th: 12th) row.
15 (15: 17: 17: 19: 19) sts.
Work 11 (9: 7: 5: 5: 9) rows, ending with a WS row.

Join sections
Next row (RS): (Inc in first st) 1 (0: 0: 0: 0: 0) times, moss st to last 5 sts of back cuff section, holding WS of front cuff section against RS of back cuff section, P tog next st of back section with first st of front section, *K tog next st of back section with next st of front section, P tog next st of back section with next st of front section, rep from * once more, then moss st to last 1 (0: 0: 0: 0: 0) st of front cuff section, (inc in last st) 1 (0: 0: 0: 0: 0) times.
39 (39: 41: 43: 45: 45) sts.
Complete as given for right sleeve from **.

MAKING UP
Press all pieces with a warm iron over a damp cloth.
Join both shoulder seams using back stitch or mattress stitch if preferred.

Collar
With RS facing and using 4½mm (US 7) needles, slip 8 (9: 9: 9: 9: 9) sts on right front holder onto right needle, rejoin yarn and pick up and knit 16 (16: 16: 18: 18: 18) sts up right side of neck, 25 (27: 27: 29: 29: 29) sts from back placing markers on first and last of these sts, and 16 (16: 16: 18: 18: 18) sts down left side of neck, then moss st 8 (9: 9: 9: 9: 9) sts on left front holder. 73 [77: 77: 83: 83: 83) sts.

Keeping moss st correct as set by sts from front neck holders, cont as folls:
Work 1 row, ending with a WS row.
Row 2 (RS): *Moss st to within 1 st of marked st, work 3 tog (marked st is centre st of these 3 sts), rep from * once more, moss st to end. 69 (73: 73: 79: 79: 79) sts.
Work 3 rows.
Change to 3¾mm (US 5) needles.
Row 6: As row 2. 65 (69: 69: 75: 75: 75) sts.
Work 3 rows.
Row 10: As row 2.
61 (65: 65: 71: 71: 71) sts.
Work 4 rows, ending with a RS row.
Cast off in moss st (on **WS**).
Join side seams. Join sleeve seams. Insert sleeves into armholes. Sew on 9 buttons to left front opening edge. Using photograph as a guide, sew 5 buttons onto each cuff, attaching buttons through both layers.

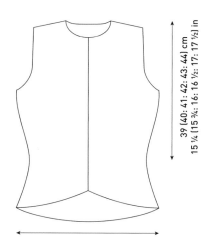

39 (40: 41: 42: 43: 44) cm
15¼ (15¾: 16: 16½: 17: 17½) in

41.5 (44: 46.5: 49: 51.5: 55.5) cm
16¼ (17¼: 18¼: 19¼: 20: 22) in

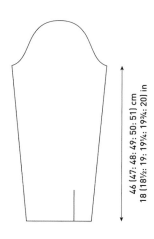

46 (47: 48: 49: 50: 51) cm
18 (18½: 19: 19¼: 19¾: 20) in

Recommendation

Suitable for the knitter with a little experience
Please see pages 18 & 19 for photographs.

	XS	S	M	L	XL	XXL	
To fit	**81**	**86**	**91**	**97**	**102**	**109**	**cm**
bust	32	34	36	38	40	43	in

Rowan by Amy Butler Sweet Harmony

| | 5 | 6 | 6 | 7 | 7 | 8 x 100gm |

Photographed in Frost

Needles

1 pair 8mm (no 0) (US 11) needles
1 pair 15mm (US 19) needles

Tension

7 sts and 10½ rows to 10 cm measured over
pattern using a combination of 8mm (US 11)
and 15mm (US 19) needles.

FOX
Skimming open stitch sweater

BACK and FRONT (both alike)

Cast on 37 (39: 41: 43: 45: 47) sts using
15mm (US 19) needles.
Row 1 (RS): Using a 8mm (US 11) needle, purl.
Row 2: Using a 15mm (US 19) needle, knit.
These 2 rows form patt.
Work in patt for a further 14 rows, ending with
a WS row.
Next row (RS): P2, P2tog, P to last 4 sts,
P2tog tbl, P2.
Working all side seam decreases as set by
last row, dec 1 st at each end of 6th and
2 foll 6th rows. 29 (31: 33: 35: 37: 39) sts.
Work 11 rows, ending with a WS row.
Next row (RS): P3, M1 purlwise, P to last
3 sts, M1 purlwise, P3.
Working increases as set by last row, inc 1 st
at each end of foll 6th row.
33 (35: 37: 39: 41: 43) sts.
Cont straight until work measures 55 (55: 56:
56: 56: 56) cm, ending with a WS row.

Shape armholes

Keeping patt correct, cast off 2 sts at beg of
next 2 rows. 29 (31: 33: 35: 37: 39) sts.
Dec 1 st at each end of next 1 (1: 1: 1: 3: 3)
rows, then on foll 1 (1: 2: 2: 1: 2) alt rows,
then on 0 (1: 1: 1: 1: 1) foll 4th row.
25 (25: 25: 27: 27: 27) sts.
Cont straight until armhole measures 18 (19:
19: 20: 21: 22) cm, ending with a WS row.

Shape shoulders

Cast off 2 sts at beg of next row.
Cast off rem sts (on **WS**), placing marker after 2nd
cast-off st (to denote other side of neck opening).

SLEEVES (both alike)

Cast on 17 (17: 17: 19: 19: 19) sts using
15mm (US 19) needles.
Beg with row 1 and working all increases in
same way as side seam increases, work in
patt as given for back and front, shaping
sides by inc 1 st at each end of 13th and
3 foll 12th rows. 25 (25: 25: 27: 27: 27) sts.
Cont straight until sleeve measures 52 (53: 54:
55: 56: 57) cm, ending with a WS row.

Shape top

Keeping patt correct, cast off 2 sts at beg of
next 2 rows. 21 (21: 21: 23: 23: 23) sts.
Dec 1 st at each end of next and 2 foll 4th
rows, then on every foll alt row until 11 sts rem,

then on foll row, ending with a WS row.
Cast off rem 9 sts.

MAKING UP

Press all pieces with a warm iron over
a damp cloth.
Join both shoulder seams using back stitch
or mattress stitch if preferred.
Join side seams. Join sleeve seams. Insert
sleeves into armholes.

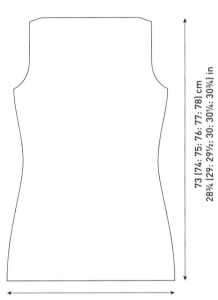

73 [74: 75: 76: 77: 78] cm
28¾ [29: 29½: 30: 30¼: 30¾] in

45.5 (48: 50.5: 53: 55.5: 59.5) cm
18 (19: 20: 21: 22: 23½) in

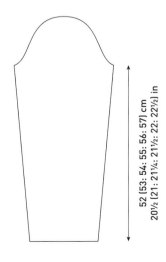

52 [53: 54: 55: 56: 57] cm
20½ [21: 21¼: 21½: 22: 22½) in

WARRIOR

Cocoon like sweater with travelling cables

Recommendation

Suitable for the knitter with a little experience
Please see page 13 for photograph.

	XS	S	M	L	XL	XXL	
To fit	81	86	91	97	102	109	cm
bust	32	34	36	38	40	43	in

Rowan Cocoon

| | 10 | 11 | 11 | 12 | 12 | 13 x 100gm |

Photographed in Scree

Needles

1 pair 6mm (no 4) (US 10) needles
1 pair 7mm (no 2) (US 10½) needles
Cable needle

Tension

15 sts and 20 rows to 10 cm measured over double moss st using 7mm (US 10½) needles.

Special abbreviations

C8B = slip next 4 sts onto cable needle and leave at back of work, K4, then K4 from cable needle.

C8F = slip next 4 sts onto cable needle and leave at front of work, K4, then K4 from cable needle.

BACK

Cast on 67 (71: 75: 79: 83: 89) sts using 7mm (US 10½) needles.

Row 1 (RS): K0 (0: 0: 1: 1: 0), (P1, K1) 6 (7: 8: 8: 9: 11) times, *P1, (inc in next st, K1) twice, inc in next st*, rep from * to * once more, (P1, K1) 9 (9: 9: 10: 10: 10) times, rep from * to * twice more, P1, (K1, P1) 6 (7: 8: 8: 9: 11) times, K0 (0: 0: 1: 1: 0).
79 (83: 87: 91: 95: 101) sts.

Row 2: K0 (0: 0: 1: 1: 0), (P1, K1) 6 (7: 8: 8: 9: 11) times, *(K1, P8) twice, K1*, K1, (P1, K1) 8 (8: 8: 9: 9: 9) times, rep from * to * once more, (K1, P1) 6 (7: 8: 8: 9: 11) times, K0 (0: 0: 1: 1: 0).

Now work in patt as folls:

Row 1 (RS): P0 (0: 0: 1: 1: 0), (K1, P1) 6 (7: 8: 8: 9: 11) times, *(P1, K8) twice, P1*, P1, (K1, P1) 8 (8: 8: 9: 9: 9) times, rep from * to * once more, (P1, K1) 6 (7: 8: 8: 9: 11) times, P0 (0: 0: 1: 1: 0).

Row 2: P0 (0: 0: 1: 1: 0), (K1, P1) 6 (7: 8: 8: 9: 11) times, *(K1, P8) twice, K1*, P1, (K1, P1) 8 (8: 8: 9: 9: 9) times, rep from * to * once more, (P1, K1) 6 (7: 8: 8: 9: 11) times, P0 (0: 0: 1: 1: 0).

Row 3: K0 (0: 0: 1: 1: 0), (P1, K1) 6 (7: 8: 8: 9: 11) times, *(P1, K8) twice, P1*, K1, (P1, K1) 8 (8: 8: 9: 9: 9) times, rep from * to * once more, (K1, P1) 6 (7: 8: 8: 9: 11) times, K0 (0: 0: 1: 1: 0).

Row 4: K0 (0: 0: 1: 1: 0), (P1, K1) 6 (7: 8: 8: 9: 11) times, *(K1, P8) twice, K1*, K1, (P1, K1) 8 (8: 8: 9: 9: 9) times, rep from * to * once more, (K1, P1) 6 (7: 8: 8: 9: 11) times, K0 (0: 0: 1: 1: 0).

Rows 5 to 8: As rows 1 to 4.

Rows 9 and 10: As rows 1 and 2.

Counting in from both ends of last row, place markers after 31st (33rd: 35th: 36th: 38th: 41st) sts in from ends of row - there should be 17 (17: 17: 19: 19: 19) sts between markers.

Row 11: Inc in first st, K1 (1: 1: 0: 0: 1), (P1, K1) 5 (6: 7: 8: 9: 10) times, *P1, C8B, P1, C8F, P1*, slip marker onto right needle, M1, K1, (P1, K1) 8 (8: 8: 9: 9: 9) times, M1, slip marker onto right needle, rep from * to * once more, (K1, P1) 5 (6: 7: 8: 9: 10) times, K1 (1: 1: 0: 0: 1), inc in last st.
83 (87: 91: 95: 99: 105) sts.

Row 12: K1 (1: 1: 0: 0: 1), (P1, K1) 6 (7: 8: 9: 10: 11) times, *(K1, P8) twice, K1*, slip marker onto right needle, (P1, K1) 9 (9: 9: 10: 10: 10) times, P1, slip marker onto right needle, rep from * to * once more, (K1, P1) 6 (7: 8: 9: 10: 11) times, K1 (1: 1: 0: 0: 1).

These 12 rows start shaping and form patt - 2 cable panels with double moss st between and at sides.

Taking markers up work (by slipping marker from left needle to right needle) and taking all inc sts into double moss st, cont as folls:
Work 10 rows, ending with a WS row.

**Row 23: Patt to marker, slip marker onto right needle, M1, patt to next marker, M1, slip marker onto right needle, patt to end.
85 (89: 93: 97: 101: 107) sts.
Work 11 rows.

Row 35: Inc in first st, patt to marker, slip marker onto right needle, M1, patt to next marker, M1, slip marker onto right needle, patt to last st, inc in last st.
89 (93: 97: 101: 105: 111) sts.
Work 11 rows.
Rep from ** once more.
95 (99: 103: 107: 111: 117) sts.
Now rep rows 23 to 34 twice more, and row 23 again. 101 (105: 109: 113: 117: 123) sts.
Work 3 (3: 5: 5: 5: 5) rows, ending with a WS row. (Back should measure 50 (50: 51: 51: 51: 51) cm.)

Shape armholes

Keeping patt correct, cast off 6 sts at beg of next 2 rows. 89 (93: 97: 101: 105: 111) sts.
Work 6 (6: 4: 4: 4: 4) rows, ending with a WS row.

Next row: As row 23.
91 (95: 99: 103: 107: 113) sts.
Work 11 rows.

Next row: As row 23.
93 (97: 101: 105: 109: 115) sts.
All shaping is now complete - remove markers.
Cont straight until armhole measures 21 (22: 22: 23: 24: 25) cm, ending with a WS row.

Shape shoulders and back neck

(**Note**: When casting off across top of cables, dec 3 sts at top of each cable to ensure shoulder seam does not stretch too much. St counts given do NOT include any decreased sts and relate to original number of sts.)

Keeping patt correct, cast off 8 (9: 9: 10: 10: 11) sts at beg of next 4 rows.
61 (61: 65: 65: 69: 71) sts.

Next row (RS): Cast off 9 (9: 10: 10: 10: 11) sts, patt until there are 13 (13: 14: 13: 15: 15) sts on right needle and turn, leaving rem sts on a holder.

Work each side of neck separately.

Cast off 4 sts at beg of next row.

Cast off rem 9 (9: 10: 9: 11: 11) sts.

With RS facing, rejoin yarn to rem sts, cast off centre 17 (17: 17: 19: 19: 19) sts, patt to end.

Complete to match first side, reversing shapings.

FRONT

Work as given for back until 8 (8: 8: 10: 10: 10) rows less have been worked than on back to start of shoulder shaping, ending with a WS row.

Shape front neck

Next row (RS): Patt 39 (41: 43: 45: 47: 50) sts and turn, leaving rem sts on a holder.

Work each side of neck separately.

Keeping patt correct, dec 1 st at neck edge of next 2 rows, then on foll 2 (2: 2: 3: 3: 3) alt rows.

35 (37: 39: 40: 42: 45) sts.

Work 1 row, ending with a WS row.

Shape shoulder

Cast off 8 (9: 9: 10: 10: 11) sts at beg of next and foll alt row, then 9 (9: 10: 10: 10: 11) sts at beg of foll alt row **and at same time** dec 1 st at neck edge of next row.

Work 1 row.

Cast off rem 9 (9: 10: 9: 11: 11) sts.

With RS facing, rejoin yarn to rem sts, cast off centre 15 sts, patt to end.

Complete to match first side, reversing shapings.

SLEEVES (both alike)

Cast on 33 (35: 35: 37: 39: 39) sts using 7mm (US 10½) needles.

Row 1 (RS): K1, *P1, K1, rep from * to end.

Row 2: As row 1.

Row 3: P1, *K1, P1, rep from * to end.

Row 4: As row 3.

These 4 rows form double moss st.

Cont in double moss st, shaping sides by inc 1 st at each end of next and every foll 4th row to 51 (57: 55: 55: 61: 65) sts, then on every foll 6th row until there are 65 (69: 69: 71: 75: 77) sts, taking inc sts into patt.

Cont straight until sleeve measures 47 (48: 49: 50: 51: 52) cm, ending with a WS row.

Cast off.

MAKING UP

Press all pieces with a warm iron over a damp cloth.

Join right shoulder seam using back stitch or mattress stitch if preferred.

Neckband

With RS facing and using 6mm (US 10) needles, pick up and knit 14 (14: 14: 16: 16: 16) sts down left side of neck, 15 sts from front, 14 (14: 14: 16: 16: 16) sts up right side of neck, then 29 (29: 29: 30: 30: 30) sts from back.
72 (72: 72: 77: 77: 77) sts.

Row 1 (WS): K2, *P3, K2, rep from * to end.

Row 2: P2, *K3, P2, rep from * to end.

These 2 rows form rib.

Cont in rib until neckband measures 12 cm, ending with a WS row.

Cast off in rib.

Join left shoulder and neckband seam.

Mark points along row-end edges of sleeves 4 cm down from cast-off edges.

Matching these marked points to top of side seams and centre of sleeve cast-off edges to shoulder seams, sew sleeves to back and front.

Join side and sleeve seams.

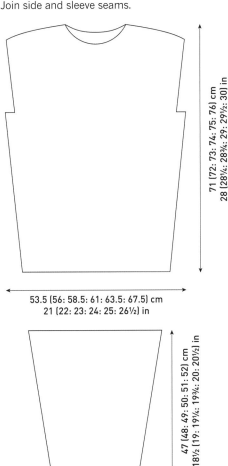

71 (72: 73: 74: 75: 76) cm
28 (28¼: 28¾: 29: 29½: 30) in

53.5 (56: 58.5: 61: 63.5: 67.5) cm
21 (22: 23: 24: 25: 26½) in

47 (48: 49: 50: 51: 52) cm
18½ (19: 19¼: 19¾: 20: 20½) in

SHEARLING
Snug waistcoat with asymmetric fronts

Recommendation

Suitable for the knitter with a little experience
Please see pages 14 & 15 for photographs.

	XS-S	M-L	XL-XXL	
To fit	81-86	91-97	102-109	cm
bust	32-34	36-38	40-43	in

Rowan Boucle

| | 6 | 7 | 8 | x 100gm |

Photographed in Light Brown Masham

Needles

1 pair 15mm (US 19) needles

Tension

10 sts and 10 rows to 10 cm measured over
pattern using 15mm (US 19) needles.

Pattern note: The number of sts varies whilst
working patt. On every WS row the number of
sts is halved, and on every RS row the number
of sts is doubled. St counts given relate to the
actual number of sts there are on needles at
that time.

BACK

Cast on 46 (52: 58) sts using 15mm (US 19)
needles.
Row 1 (WS): P2tog, *K2tog, P2tog, rep from
* to end.
23 (26: 29) sts.
Row 2: Inc once (by knitting into front and
back of st) in each st to end.
46 (52: 58) sts.
These 2 rows form patt.
Cont straight until back measures approx
35 (36: 36) cm, ending with a WS row.
23 (26: 29) sts.

Shape armholes

Row 1 (RS): K2, lift 2nd st on right needle
over first st and off right needle - one st cast
off, inc in next st, lift 3rd st on right needle
over first and 2nd sts and off right needle -
2nd st cast off, patt to end.
42 (48: 54) sts.
Row 2: P2tog, K2tog, lift 2nd st on right
needle over first st and off right needle - one
st cast off, P2tog, lift 2nd st on right needle
over first st and off right needle - 2nd st cast
off, patt
to end.
19 (22: 25) sts.
Work 4 rows.
Row 7: Inc once in each of first 2 sts, *K3tog
leaving sts on left needle, then K3tog tbl into
same 3 sts and let these 3 sts slip off left
needle*, inc once in each st to last 5 sts, rep
from * to * once more, inc once in each of
last 2 sts.
30 (36: 42) sts.

Size M-L only

Work 3 rows. 18 sts.
Row 11: Inc once in each of first 2 sts, *K2tog
leaving sts on left needle, then K2tog tbl into
same 2 sts and let these 2 sts slip off left
needle*, inc once in each st to last 4 sts, rep
from * to * once more, inc once in each of
last 2 sts. 32 sts.

Size XL-XXL only

Work 3 rows. 21 sts.
Row 11: As row 7. 34 sts.

All sizes

Cont straight until armhole measures approx
20 (21: 23) cm, ending with a WS row.
15 (16: 17) sts.

Shape shoulders

Next row (RS): (K2, lift 2nd st on right
needle over first st and off right needle
- one st cast off) twice, inc in next st, lift
3rd st on right needle over first and 2nd
sts and off right needle - 3rd st cast off,
patt to end. 24 (26: 28) sts.
Next row: P2tog, K2tog, lift 2nd st on
right needle over first st and off right
needle - one st cast off, *P2tog, lift 2nd
st on right needle over first st and off
right needle, K2tog, lift 2nd st on right
needle over first st and off right needle,
rep from * to end.
Fasten off, placing a marker after 3rd
cast-off st.

Pattern note: Row-end edges of fronts form
actual front opening edges. To ensure edges
remains neat and tidy, make sure yarns are
joined in at side seam edge **only**.

LEFT FRONT

Cast on 34 (38: 42) sts using 15mm (US 19)
needles.
Row 1 (WS): P2tog, *K2tog, P2tog, rep from *
to end. 17 (19: 21) sts.
Row 2: Inc once in each st to end.
34 (38: 42) sts.
These 2 rows form patt.
Now shape lower edge as folls:
Row 3: P2tog, K2tog, P2tog, wrap next st
(by slipping next st from left needle onto
right needle, taking yarn to opposite side
of work between needles and then slipping
same st back onto left needle - when
working back across wrapped sts work
the wrapped st and the wrapping loop
tog as one st) and turn.
Row 4: Inc once in each st to end.
Row 5: P2tog, (K2tog, P2tog) 3 times,
wrap next st and turn.
Row 6: Inc once in each st to end.
Row 7: P2tog, (K2tog, P2tog) 6 times,
wrap next st and turn.
Row 8: Inc once in each st to end.
Now cont in patt across all sts until shorter
row-end edge measures approx 35 (36: 36)
cm, ending with a WS row.
17 (19: 21) sts.

Shape armhole

Row 1 (RS): K2, lift 2nd st on right needle over first st and off right needle - one st cast off, inc in next st, lift 3rd st on right needle over first and 2nd sts and off right needle - 2nd st cast off, patt to end.
30 (34: 38) sts.
Work 5 rows. 15 (17: 19) sts.

Row 7: Inc once in each of first 2 sts, K3tog leaving sts on left needle, then K3tog tbl into same 3 sts and let these 3 sts slip off left needle, inc once in each st to end.
26 (30: 34) sts.

Size M-L only

Work 3 rows. 15 sts.

Row 11: Inc once in each of first 2 sts, K2tog leaving sts on left needle, then K2tog tbl into same 2 sts and let these 2 sts slip off left needle, inc once in each st to end. 28 sts.

Size XL-XXL only

Work 3 rows. 17 sts.

Row 11: As row 7. 30 sts.

All sizes

Cont straight until armhole measures approx 20 (21: 23) cm, ending with a WS row.
13 (14: 15) sts.

Shape shoulders

Next row (RS): (K2, lift 2nd st on right needle over first st and off right needle - one st cast off) twice, inc in next st, lift 3rd st on right needle over first and 2nd sts and off right needle - 3rd st cast off, patt to end.
20 (22: 24) sts.
Cont in patt on these sts for a further 8 (10: 10) rows for back neck border extension, ending with a RS row.

Next row (WS): P2tog, (K2tog, P2tog) twice, wrap next st and turn.

Next row: Patt to end.
Cast off.

RIGHT FRONT

Cast on 34 (38: 42) sts using 15mm (US 19) needles.

Row 1 (WS): P2tog, *K2tog, P2tog, rep from * to end. 17 (19: 21) sts.
This row sets position of patt as given for back and left front.
Now shape lower edge as folls:

Row 2: Inc once in each of first 3 sts, wrap next st and turn.

Row 3: Patt to end.

Row 4: Inc once in each of first 6 sts, wrap next st and turn.

Row 5: Patt to end.

Row 6: Inc once in each of first 9 sts, wrap next st and turn.

Row 7: Patt to end.

Row 8: Inc once in each of first 12 sts, wrap next st and turn.

Row 9: Patt to end.

Row 10: Inc once in each of first 15 sts, wrap next st and turn.

Row 11: Patt to end.
Now cont in patt across all sts until shorter row-end edge measures approx 35 (36: 36) cm, ending with a RS row.
34 (38: 42) sts.
Complete to match left front, reversing all shaping.

MAKING UP

Press all pieces with a warm iron over a damp cloth.
Join both shoulder seams using back stitch or mattress stitch if preferred. Join cast-off edges of back neck border extensions, then sew row-end edge in place to back neck edge.
Join side seams.

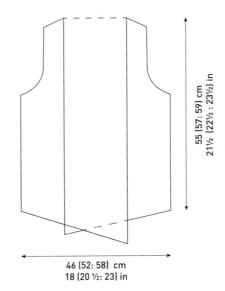

55 (57: 59) cm
21½ (22½ : 23½) in

46 (52: 58) cm
18 (20 ½: 23) in

HAWK

Edge to edge jacket with bobbled cuffs

Recommendation

Suitable for the knitter with a little experience
Please see page 16 for photograph.

	XS	S	M	L	XL	XXL	
To fit	**81**	**86**	**91**	**97**	**102**	**109**	cm
bust	32	34	36	38	40	43	in

Rowan Big Wool

8 8 9 9 10 11 x 100gm
Photographed in Champion

Needles

1 pair 8mm (no 0) (US 11) needles
1 pair 10mm (no 000) (US 15) needles

Tension

10 sts and 13 rows to 10 cm measured over
pattern using 10mm (US 15) needles.

Special abbreviation

MB = make bobble as folls: (K1, P1, K1, P1,
K1) all into next st, turn, K5, turn, K5, lift 2nd,
3rd, 4th and 5th sts on right needle over first st
and off right needle.

BACK

Cast on 47 (49: 51: 55: 57: 61) sts using
10mm (US 15) needles.
Row 1 (RS): P0 (1: 0: 0: 1: 1), *K1 tbl, P1, rep
from * to last 1 (0: 1: 1: 0: 0) st, (K1 tbl) 1 (0:
1: 1: 0: 0) times.
Row 2: Knit.
These 2 rows form patt.
Work in patt for a further 6 rows, ending with
a WS row.
Row 9 (RS): Patt 6 (7: 8: 8: 9: 9) sts, K3tog
tbl, patt to last 9 (10: 11: 11: 12: 12) sts,
K3tog tbl, patt 6 (7: 8: 8: 9: 9) sts.
43 (45: 47: 51: 53: 57) sts.
Work 7 rows.
Row 17: As row 9.
39 (41: 43: 47: 49: 53) sts.
Work 5 rows.
Row 23: As row 9.
35 (37: 39: 43: 45: 49) sts.
Work 9 rows, ending with a WS row.
Inc 1 st at each end of next and 4 foll 4th rows,
taking inc sts into patt.
45 (47: 49: 53: 55: 59) sts.
Cont straight until back measures 42 (42: 43:
43: 43: 43) cm, ending with a WS row.

Shape armholes

Keeping patt correct, cast off 3 sts at beg of
next 2 rows. 39 (41: 43: 47: 49: 53) sts.
Dec 1 st at each end of next 1 (1: 1: 3: 3: 5)
rows, then on foll 1 (2: 2: 2: 2: 2) alt rows.
35 (35: 37: 37: 39: 39) sts.
Cont straight until armhole measures 18 (19:
19: 20: 21: 22) cm, ending with a WS row.

Shape shoulders and back neck

Next row (RS): Cast off 5 sts, patt until there
are 9 (9: 10: 9: 10: 10) sts on right needle
and turn, leaving rem sts on a holder.
Work each side of neck separately.
Cast off 4 sts at beg of next row.
Cast off rem 5 (5: 6: 5: 6: 6) sts.
With RS facing, rejoin yarn to rem sts, cast off
centre 7 (7: 7: 9: 9: 9) sts, patt to end.
Complete to match first side, reversing
shapings.

Pattern note: Row-end edges of fronts forms
actual front opening edges. To ensure edges
remains neat and tidy, make sure new balls
of yarn are joined in at side seam edges **only**.

LEFT FRONT

Cast on 27 (28: 29: 31: 32: 34) sts using
10mm (US 15) needles.
Row 1 (RS): P0 (1: 0: 0: 1: 1), *K1 tbl, P1,
rep from * to last 3 sts, (K1 tbl) 3 times.
Row 2: Knit.
These 2 rows form patt.
Work in patt for a further 6 rows, ending with
a WS row.
Row 9 (RS): Patt 6 (7: 8: 8: 9: 9) sts, K3tog
tbl, patt to end. 25 (26: 27: 29: 30: 32) sts.
Work 7 rows.
Row 17: As row 9. 23 (24: 25: 27: 28: 30) sts.
Work 5 rows.
Row 23: As row 9. 21 (22: 23: 25: 26: 28) sts.
Work 9 rows, ending with a WS row.
Inc 1 st at beg of next and 4 foll 4th rows,
taking inc sts into patt.
26 (27: 28: 30: 31: 33) sts.
Cont straight until left front matches back
to start of armhole shaping, ending with
a WS row.

Shape armhole

Keeping patt correct, cast off 3 sts at beg
of next row. 23 (24: 25: 27: 28: 30) sts.
Work 1 row.
Dec 1 st at armhole edge of next 1 (1: 1: 3: 3:
5) rows, then on foll 1 (2: 2: 2: 2: 2) alt rows.
21 (21: 22: 22: 23: 23) sts.
Cont straight until 8 (8: 8: 10: 10: 10) rows
less have been worked than on back to start
of shoulder shaping, ending with a WS row.

Shape front neck

Next row (RS): Patt 15 (15: 16: 16: 17: 17)
sts and turn, leaving rem 6 sts on a holder.
Dec 1 st at neck edge of next 4 rows, then on
foll 1 (1: 1: 2: 2: 2) alt rows.
10 (10: 11: 10: 11: 11) sts.
Work 1 row, ending with a WS row.

Shape shoulder

Cast off 5 sts at beg of next row.
Work 1 row.
Cast off rem 5 (5: 6: 5: 6: 6) sts.

RIGHT FRONT

Cast on 27 (28: 29: 31: 32: 34) sts using
10mm (US 15) needles.
Row 1 (RS): (K1 tbl) 3 times, *P1, K1 tbl,
rep from * to last 0 (1: 0: 0: 1: 1) st,
P0 (1: 0: 0: 1: 1).

Row 2: Knit.

These 2 rows form patt.

Work in patt for a further 6 rows, ending with a WS row.

Row 9 (RS): Patt to last 9 (10: 11: 11: 12: 12) sts, K3tog tbl, patt to end.

25 (26: 27: 29: 30: 32) sts.

Complete to match left front, reversing shapings and working first row of neck shaping as folls:

Shape front neck

Next row (RS): Patt 6 sts and slip these sts onto a holder, patt to end.

15 (15: 16: 16: 17: 17)) sts.

SLEEVES (both alike)

Cast on 27 (27: 29: 29: 31: 31) sts using 8mm (US 11) needles.

Row 1 (WS): Purl.

Row 2: K2 (2: 3: 3: 2: 2), *yfwd, K3tog, yfwd, MB, rep from * to last 5 (5: 6: 6: 5: 5) sts, yfwd, K3tog, yfwd, K2 (2: 3: 3: 2: 2).

Row 3: Purl.

Row 4: K1 (1: 2: 2: 1: 1), K2tog, yfwd, *MB, yfwd, K3tog, yfwd, rep from * to last 4 (4: 5: 5: 4: 4) sts, MB, yfwd, K2tog, K1 (1: 2: 2: 1: 1).

These 4 rows form bobble patt.

Work in bobble patt for a further 12 rows, ending with a **RS** row.

Row 17 (WS): Knit.

Change to 10mm (US 15) needles.

Now work in patt as given for back as folls:

Row 1 (RS): Inc in first st, *K1 tbl, P1, rep from * to last 2 sts, K1 tbl, inc in last st.

Row 2: Knit.

These 2 rows form patt and beg sleeve shaping.

Cont in patt, shaping sides by inc 1 st at each end of 16th (10th: 16th: 12th: 18th: 12th) and foll 16th (10th: 18th: 12th: 18th: 12th) row, then on foll - (12th: -: 12th: -: 14th) row, taking inc sts into patt.

33 (35: 35: 37: 37: 39) sts.

Cont straight until sleeve measures 47 (48: 49: 50: 51: 52) cm, ending with a WS row.

Shape top

Keeping patt correct, cast off 3 sts at beg of next 2 rows.

27 (29: 29: 31: 31: 33) sts.

Dec 1 st at each end of next and 2 (3: 3: 3: 3: 3) foll 4th rows, then on foll 3 (1: 1: 2: 2: 3) alt rows, then on foll 1 (3: 3: 3: 3: 3) rows, ending with a WS row.

Cast off rem 13 sts.

MAKING UP

Press all pieces with a warm iron over a damp cloth.

Join both shoulder seams using back stitch or mattress stitch if preferred.

Neckband

With RS facing and using 8mm (US 11) needles, slip 6 sts on right front holder onto right needle, rejoin yarn and pick up and knit 10 (10: 10: 12: 12: 12) sts up right side of neck, 15 (15: 15: 17: 17: 17) sts from back, and 10 (10: 10: 12: 12: 12) sts down left side of neck, then patt 6 sts on left front holder. 47 (47: 47: 53: 53: 53) sts.

Work in g st for 4 rows, ending with a **RS** row.

Cast off knitwise (on **WS**).

Join side seams. Join sleeve seams. Insert sleeves into armholes.

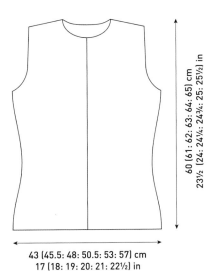

60 (61: 62: 63: 64: 65) cm
23½ (24: 24¼: 24¾: 25: 25½) in

43 (45.5: 48: 50.5: 53: 57) cm
17 (18: 19: 20: 21: 22½) in

47 (48: 49: 50: 51: 52) cm
18½ (19: 19¼: 19¾: 20) in

TRIBE
Multi striped moss stitch jacket

Recommendation
Suitable for the knitter with a little experience
Please see pages 20 & 21 for photographs.

	XS	S	M	L	XL	XXL	
To fit	81	86	91	97	102	109	cm
bust	32	34	36	38	40	43	in

Rowan Cocoon

A Shale							
	4	4	5	5	6	6	x 100gm
B Mountain							
	2	2	2	3	3	3	x 100gm
C Scree							
	2	2	2	3	3	3	x 100gm
D Alpine							
	1	1	1	1	1	1	x 100gm
E Mink							
	2	2	2	2	3	3	x 100gm
F Quarry Tile							
	1	2	2	2	2	2	x 100gm
G Bilberry							
	1	1	1	2	2	2	x 100gm

Needles
1 pair 7mm (no 2) (US 10½) needles

Tension
14 sts and 24 rows to 10 cm measured over
moss stitch using 7mm (US 10½) needles.

STRIPE SEQUENCE
Rows 1 to 16: Using yarn A.
Rows 17 to 22: Using yarn C.
Rows 23 to 26: Using yarn B.
Rows 27 to 36: Using yarn A.
Rows 37 to 42: Using yarn E.
Rows 43 and 44: Using yarn D.
Rows 45 and 46: Using yarn C.
Rows 47 to 50: Using yarn G.
Rows 51 and 52: Using yarn B.
Rows 53 to 62: Using yarn F.
Rows 63 and 64: Using yarn B.
Rows 65 to 68: Using yarn G.
Rows 69 and 70: Using yarn C.
Rows 71 and 72: Using yarn D.
Rows 73 to 78: Using yarn E.
Rows 79 to 88: Using yarn A.
Rows 89 to 92: Using yarn B.
Rows 93 to 102: Using yarn A.
Rows 103 to 108: Using yarn C.
Rows 109 and 110: Using yarn E.
Rows 111 and 112: Using yarn G.
Rows 113 to 116: Using yarn B.
Rows 117 and 118: Using yarn F.
Rows 119 to 128: Using yarn D.
Rows 129 and 130: Using yarn F.
Rows 131 to 134: Using yarn B.
Rows 135 and 136: Using yarn G.
Rows 137 and 138: Using yarn E.
Rows 139 to 144: Using yarn C.
Rows 145 to 154: Using yarn A.
Rows 155 to 158: Using yarn B.
Rows 159 to 168: Using yarn A.
Rows 169 to 174: Using yarn E.
Rows 175 and 176: Using yarn D.
Rows 177 and 178: Using yarn C.
Rows 179 to 182: Using yarn G.
Rows 183 and 184: Using yarn B.
Rows 185 to 194: Using yarn F.
Rows 195 and 196: Using yarn B.
Rows 197 to 202: Using yarn G.
These 202 rows form stripe sequence and
are repeated as required.

BACK
Cast on 69 (73: 77: 81: 85: 91) sts using
7mm (US 10½) needles and yarn A.
Beg with stripe row 1, now work in stripe
sequence (see above) in moss st as folls:
Row 1 (RS): K1, *P1, K1, rep from * to end.

Row 2: As row 1.
These 2 rows form moss st.
Cont in moss st, shaping side seams by dec
1 st at each end of 25th and 3 foll 26th rows.
61 (65: 69: 73: 77: 83) sts.
Cont straight until back measures 54 (54: 55:
55: 55: 55) cm, ending with a WS row.
Shape armholes
Keeping stripes correct, cast off 4 sts at beg
of next 2 rows.
53 (57: 61: 65: 69: 75) sts.
Dec 1 st at each end of next 1 (3: 3: 5: 5: 7)
rows, then on foll 2 (1: 2: 2: 3: 3) alt rows,
then on foll 4th row.
45 (47: 49: 49: 51: 53) sts.
Cont straight until armhole measures 19 (20:
20: 20: 21: 22: 23) cm, ending with a WS row.
Shape shoulders and back neck
Cast off 4 (5: 5: 5: 5: 5) sts at beg of next
2 rows.
37 (37: 39: 39: 41: 43) sts.
Next row (RS): Cast off 4 (5: 5: 5: 5: 5) sts,
moss st until there are 9 (8: 9: 8: 9: 10) sts
on right needle and turn, leaving rem sts
on a holder.
Work each side of neck separately.
Cast off 4 sts at beg of next row.
Cast off rem 5 (4: 5: 4: 5: 6) sts.
With RS facing, rejoin appropriate yarn to rem
sts, cast off centre 11 (11: 11: 13: 13: 13) sts,
patt to end.
Complete to match first side, reversing
shapings.

Pattern note: Row-end edge of left front forms
actual front opening edge. To ensure edge
remains neat and tidy, make sure yarns are
joined in at side seam edge **only**.

LEFT FRONT
Cast on 45 (47: 49: 51: 53: 57) sts using
7mm (US 10½) needles and yarn A.
Beg with stripe row 1, now work in stripe
sequence (see above) in moss st as given
for back as folls:
Dec 1 st at beg of 27th and 3 foll 26th rows.
41 (43: 45: 47: 49: 53) sts.
Cont straight until left front matches back
to start of armhole shaping, ending with
a WS row.

Shape armhole

Keeping stripes correct, cast off 4 sts at beg
of next row.
37 (39: 41: 43: 45: 49) sts.
Work 1 row.
Dec 1 st at armhole edge of next 1 (3: 3: 5: 5:
7) rows, then on foll 2 (1: 2: 2: 3: 3) alt rows,
then on foll 4th row.
33 (34: 35: 35: 36: 38) sts.
Cont straight until left front matches back
to start of shoulder shaping, ending with
a WS row.

Shape shoulder

Cast off 4 (5: 5: 5: 5: 5) sts at beg of next
and foll alt row, then 5 (4: 5: 4: 5: 6) sts
at beg of foll alt row.
Work a further 16 (16: 16: 18: 18: 18) rows
on these 20 (20: 20: 21: 21: 22) sts only for
back neck border extension, ending at front
opening edge.
Next row: Moss st to last 7 sts, wrap next
st (by slipping next st from left needle
onto right needle, taking yarn to opposite
side of work between needles and then
slipping same st back onto left needle
- when working back across wrapped
sts work the wrapped st and the wrapping
loop tog as one st) and turn.
Next row: Moss st to end.
Next row: Moss st to last 14 sts, wrap next
st and turn.
Next row: Moss st to end.
Work 1 row across all sts.
Cast off in moss st.

RIGHT FRONT

As fabric is totally reversible and to ensure
front opening edge remains neat and tidy,
work exactly as given for left front - but use
WS of work as RS and vice versa.

SLEEVES (both alike)

Cast on 23 (23: 25: 25: 27: 29) sts using
7mm (US 10½) needles and yarn A.
Beg with stripe row 13 (11: 11: 9: 5: 3), now
work in stripe sequence (see above) in moss
st as given for back as folls:
Inc 1 st at each end of 21st and every foll
8th row to 39 (47: 37: 45: 43: 43) sts,
then on 3 (0: 5: 2: 4: 5) foll 10th rows,
taking inc sts into striped moss st.
45 (47: 47: 49: 51: 53) sts.
Cont straight until sleeve measures
approx 49 (50: 51: 52: 53: 54) cm,
ending after same stripe row as on
back to beg of armhole shaping and
with a WS row.

Shape top

Keeping stripes correct, cast off 4 sts at beg
of next 2 rows.
37 (39: 39: 41: 43: 45) sts.
Dec 1 st at each end of next and 6 foll
4th rows, then on every foll alt row until
21 sts rem, then on foll 3 rows, ending
with a WS row.
Cast off rem 15 sts.

MAKING UP

Press all pieces with a warm iron over
a damp cloth.
Join both shoulder seams using back stitch
or mattress stitch if preferred. Join cast-off
edges of back neck border extensions, then
sew row-end edge in place to back neck edge.
Join side seams. Join sleeve seams. Insert
sleeves into armholes.

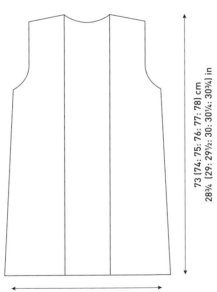

73 (74: 75: 76: 77: 78) cm
28¾ (29: 29½: 30: 30¼: 30¾) in

43.5 (46.5: 49: 52: 55: 59.5) cm
17 (18¼: 19¼: 20½: 21¾: 22¼) in

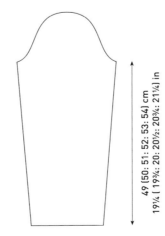

49 (50: 51: 52: 53: 54) cm
19¼ (19¾: 20: 20½: 20¾: 21¼) in

BLAZE
Semi-fitted aran sweater

Recommendation

Suitable for the knitter with a little experience
Please see pages 23, 24 & 25 for photographs.

	XS	S	M	L	XL	XXL	
To fit	**81**	**86**	**91**	**97**	**102**	**109**	cm
bust	32	34	36	38	40	43	in

Rowan Kid Classic and Kidsilk Haze

A Kid Classic

    7   7   8   8   9   9   x 50gm

B Kidsilk Haze

    4   4   5   5   5   6   x 25gm

Photographed in Kid Classic in Victoria and
Kidsilk Haze in Liqueur

Needles

1 pair 5mm (no 6) (US 8) needles
1 pair 6mm (no 4) (US 10) needles
Cable needle

Tension

16 sts and 20 rows to 10 cm measured over
stocking stitch using 6mm (US 10) needles
and one strand each of yarns A and B held
together.

Special abbreviations

C2B = slip next st onto cn and leave at back
of work, K1, then K1 from cn; **C2F** = slip next
st onto cn and leave at front of work, K1, then
K1 from cn; **C4B** = slip next 2 sts onto cn and
leave at back of work, K2, then K2 from cn;
C4F = slip next 2 sts onto cn and leave at front
of work, K2, then K2 from cn; **C8B** = slip next
4 sts onto cn and leave at back of work, K4,
then K4 from cn; **C8F** = slip next 4 sts onto cn
and leave at front of work, K4, then K4 from cn;
cn = cable needle.

BACK and FRONT (both alike)

Cast on 74 (78: 82: 86: 90: 96) sts
using 5mm (US 8) needles and one
strand each of yarns A and B held
together.
Row 1 (RS): K0 (0: 0: 0: 0: 1), P0 (2: 0: 2: 0:
2), *K2, P2, rep from * to last 2 (0: 2: 0: 2: 1)
sts, K2 (0: 2: 0: 2: 1).
Row 2: P0 (0: 0: 0: 0: 1), K0 (2: 0: 2: 0: 2),
*P2, K2, rep from * to last 2 (0: 2: 0: 2: 1) sts,
P2 (0: 2: 0: 2: 1).
These 2 rows form rib.
Work in rib for a further 9 rows, ending
with a **RS** row.
Row 12 (WS): Rib 12 (14: 16: 18: 20: 23),
M1, (rib 2, M1, rib 4, M1) 3 times, (rib 1,
M1) 13 times, rib 5, M1, rib 2, M1, (rib 4,
M1, rib 2, M1) twice, rib 12 (14: 16: 18:
20: 23).
100 (104: 108: 112: 116: 122) sts.
Change to 6mm (US 10) needles.
Beg and ending rows as indicated and rep
the 12 row patt rep throughout, cont in
patt from chart for body as folls:
Dec 1 st at each end of 3rd and 2 foll 6th rows,
then on 2 foll 4th rows.
90 (94: 98: 102: 106: 112) sts.
Work 9 rows, ending with a WS row.
Inc 1 st at each end of next and 5 foll 6th rows,
taking inc sts into patt.
102 (106: 110: 114: 118: 124) sts.
Work 5 (5: 7: 7: 7: 7) rows, ending with
a WS row.
(Work should measure approx 38 (38: 39:
39: 39: 39) cm.)
Shape raglan armholes
Keeping patt correct, cast off 6 sts at beg
of next 2 rows.
90 (94: 98: 102: 106: 112) sts.
Dec 1 st at each end of next 1 (1: 5: 5: 7: 11)
rows, then on foll 11 (12: 10: 11: 11: 10) alt
rows, ending with a **RS** row.
66 (68: 68: 70: 70: 70) sts.
Next row (WS): P0 (0: 0: 1: 1: 1), K1 (2: 2:
2: 2: 2), P1, P2tog, P2, P2tog tbl, P1, K2,
P2tog, P2tog tbl, K2, (P2tog, P2tog tbl) 8
times, K2, P2tog, P2tog tbl, K2, P1, P2tog,
P2, P2tog tbl, P1, K1 (2: 2: 2: 2: 2), P0 (0:
0: 1: 1: 1).
Cast off rem 42 (44: 44: 46: 46: 46) sts.

SLEEVES (both alike)

Cast on 42 (44: 44: 46: 48: 50) sts using
5mm (US 8) needles and one strand each
of yarns A and B held together.
Row 1 (RS): K0 (0: 0: 0: 1: 0), P0 (1: 1: 2: 2:
0), *K2, P2, rep from * to last 2 (3: 3: 0: 1: 2)
sts, K2 (2: 2: 0: 1: 2), P0 (1: 1: 0: 0: 0).
Row 2: P0 (0: 0: 0: 1: 0), K0 (1: 1: 2: 2: 0),
*P2, K2, rep from * to last 2 (3: 3: 0: 1: 2) sts,
P2 (2: 2: 0: 1: 2), K0 (1: 1: 0: 0: 0).
These 2 rows form rib.
Work in rib for a further 9 rows, ending with
a **RS** row.
Row 12 (WS): Inc in first st, rib 7 (8: 8: 9: 10:
11), (M1, rib 2, M1, rib 4) 4 times, M1, rib 2,
M1, rib 7 (8: 8: 9: 10: 11), inc in last st.
54 (56: 56: 58: 60: 62) sts.
Change to 6mm (US 10) needles.
Beg and ending rows as indicated and rep the
12 row patt rep throughout, cont in patt from
chart for sleeve as folls:
Inc 1 st at each end of 11th and 3 (4: 4: 4: 3:
2) foll 10th rows, then on 1 (-: -: -: 1: 2) foll 8th
(-: -: -: 12th: 12th) rows, taking inc sts into patt.
64 (66: 66: 68: 70: 72) sts.
Work 7 (7: 9: 11: 11: 11) rows, ending with
a WS row. (Sleeve should measure approx 33
(34: 35: 36: 37: 38) cm.)
Shape raglan
Keeping patt correct, cast off 6 sts at beg of
next 2 rows. 52 (54: 54: 56: 58: 60) sts.
Dec 1 st at each end of next and foll 11 (12:
12: 13: 14: 15) alt rows, ending with a **RS** row.
28 sts.
Next row (WS): K2, P1, P2tog, P2, P2tog tbl,
P1, K2, P2tog, P2tog tbl, K2, P1, P2tog, P2,
P2tog tbl, P1, K2.
Cast off rem 22 sts.

MAKING UP

Press all pieces with a warm iron over
a damp cloth.
Join both front and right back raglan seams
using back stitch or mattress stitch if preferred.
Neckband
With RS facing and using 5mm (US 8) needles,
pick up and knit 1 st from top of back edge
of left sleeve, place marker on needle, then
a further 22 sts from top of left sleeve, place
marker on needle, 40 (42: 42: 44: 44: 44) sts

from front, place marker on needle, 22 sts
from top of right sleeve, place marker on
needle, 40 (42: 42: 44: 44: 44) sts from back,
place marker on needle, then 1 more st from
top of left sleeve edge of back.
126 (130: 130: 134: 134: 134) sts, 5 markers
in total.

Row 1 (WS): P1, *slip marker onto right
needle, P1, K2, P0 (1: 1: 2: 2: 2), (K2, P2)
8 times, K2, P0 (1: 1: 2: 2: 2), K2, P1, slip
marker onto right needle, P1, K2, P1, (K2,
P2) 3 times, (K2, P1) twice, rep from * once
more, P1.
This row sets position of rib as given for back
and front.
Keeping rib correct as now set, cont as folls:

Row 2: K1, (slip marker onto right needle, K1,
P1, P2tog, rib to within 4 sts of next marker,
P2tog, P1, K1) 4 times, slip marker onto right
needle, K1.
118 (122: 122: 126: 126: 126) sts.

Row 3: P1, (slip marker onto right needle, P1,
K2, rib to within 3 sts of next marker, K2, P1)
4 times, slip marker onto right needle, P1.

Row 4: K1, (slip marker onto right needle, K1,
P2, rib to within 3 sts of next marker, P2, K1)
4 times, slip marker onto right needle, K1.

Row 5: As row 3.

Row 6: As row 2.
110 (114: 114: 118: 118: 118) sts.

Row 7: As row 3.

Row 8: As row 2.
102 (106: 106: 110: 110: 110) sts.
Cast off in rib (on WS).
Join left back raglan and neckband seam. Join
side and sleeve seams.

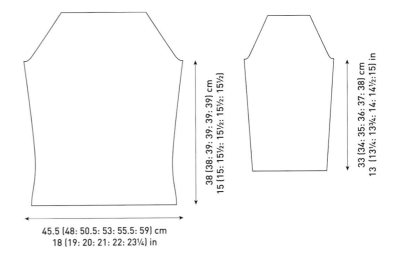

45.5 (48: 50.5: 53: 55.5: 59) cm
18 (19: 20: 21: 22: 23¼) in

38 (38: 39: 39: 39: 39) cm
15 (15: 15½: 15½: 15½: 15½) in

33 (34: 35: 36: 37: 38) cm
13 (13¼: 13¾: 14: 14½: 15) in

KEY

□ K on RS, P on WS	⧄ C4B
▪ P on RS, K on WS	⧅ C4F
⊍ K1 tbl	C8B
⧄ C2B	C8F
⧅ C2F	

Sleeve chart

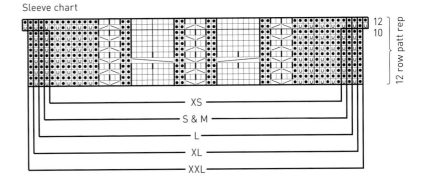

12 row patt rep

XS
S & M
L
XL
XXL

Body chart

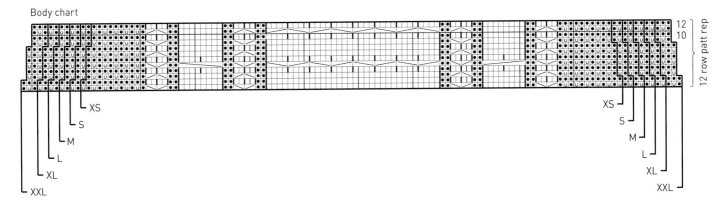

12 row patt rep

XS
S
M
L
XL
XXL

XS
S
M
L
XL
XXL

RUMOUR

Cardigan & sweater with softly gathered hemline

Recommendation

Suitable for the knitter with a little experience
Please see pages 26 to 29 for photographs.

	XS	S	M	L	XL	XXL	
To fit	81	86	91	97	102	109	cm
bust	32	34	36	38	40	43	in

Rowan Kidsilk Haze
Sweater

	5	5	6	6	7	7	x 25gm

Cardigan

	5	6	7	7	8	8	x 25gm

Sweater photographed in Shadow, cardigan in Blackcurrant

Needles

1 pair 2¾mm (no 12) (US 2) needles
1 pair 3¼mm (no 10) (US 3) needles
Sweater only: 2.50mm (no 12) (US C2) crochet hook

Buttons - 6 for sweater, and 6 for cardigan

Tension

25 sts and 34 rows to 10 cm measured over st st using 3¼mm (US 3) needles.

Sweater

Crochet abbreviations

dc = double crochet; **ch** = chain.

FRONT

Cast on 324 (344: 364: 384: 404: 434) sts using 3¼mm (US 3) needles.
Row 1 (RS): *K2, lift 2nd st on right needle over first st and off right needle, rep from * to end.
162 (172: 182: 192: 202: 217) sts.
Starting with a P row, work in st st for 45 rows, ending with a WS row.
Place markers at both ends of last row.
Row 47 (RS): K1 (1: 1: 1: 1: 2), *K2tog, K1, K2tog, rep from * to last 1 (1: 1: 1: 1: 5) sts, (K2tog) 0 (0: 0: 0: 0: 1) times, K1 (1: 1: 1: 1: 3).
98 (104: 110: 116: 122: 132) sts.
Work 13 rows.
Row 61 (RS): K3, M1, K to last 3 sts, M1, K3.
Working all side seam increases as set by last row, inc 1 st at each end of 14th and 3 foll 14th rows.
108 (114: 120: 126: 132: 142) sts.
Work 17 (17: 21: 21: 21: 21) rows, ending with a WS row. (Work should measure 26 (26: 27: 27: 27: 27) cm **from markers.**)
Shape armholes
Cast off 5 (5: 6: 6: 7: 7) sts at beg of next 2 rows. 98 (104: 108: 114: 118: 128) sts.
Dec 1 st at each end of next 5 (5: 7: 7: 9: 11) rows, then on foll 2 (4: 3: 4: 3: 4) alt rows, then on foll 4th row. 82 (84: 86: 90: 92: 96) sts.**
Cont straight until armhole measures 18 (19: 19: 20: 21: 22) cm, ending with a WS row.
Shape shoulders
Cast off 5 (5: 5: 6: 6: 7) sts at beg of next 4 rows, then 5 (5: 6: 5: 6: 6) sts at beg of foll 2 rows. 52 (54: 54: 56: 56: 56) sts.
Work a further 10 rows on these sts for funnel neck, ending with a WS row.
Cast off loosely.

BACK

Work as given for front to **.
Cont straight until 40 rows less have been worked than on front to start of shoulder shaping, ending with a WS row.
Divide for back opening
Next row (RS): K41 (42: 43: 45: 46: 48) and turn, leaving rem sts on a holder.
Work each side of neck separately.
Work 39 rows, ending with a WS row.

Shape shoulder
Cast off 5 (5: 5: 6: 6: 7) sts at beg of next and foll alt row, then 5 (5: 6: 5: 6: 6) sts at beg of foll alt row. 26 (27: 27: 28: 28: 28) sts.
Work a further 11 rows on these sts for funnel neck, ending with a WS row.
Cast off loosely.
With RS facing, rejoin yarn to rem sts, K to end.
Complete to match first side, reversing shapings.

SLEEVES (both alike)

Cast on 108 (112: 116: 124: 128: 132) sts using 3¼mm (US 3) needles.
Row 1 (RS): *K2, lift 2nd st on right needle over first st and off right needle, rep from * to end. 54 (56: 58: 62: 64: 66) sts.
Starting with a P row and working all sleeve increases in same way as side seam increases, now work in st st, shaping sides by inc 1 st at each end of 12th (14th: 14th: 16th: 14th: 14th) and every foll 12th (14th: 14th: 16th: 14th: 14th) row to 58 (78: 78: 82: 76: 76) sts, then on every foll 14th (-: 16th: -: 16th: 16th) row until there are 76 (-: 80: -: 86: 88) sts.
Cont straight until sleeve measures 49 (50: 51: 52: 53: 54) cm, ending with a WS row.
Shape top
Cast off 5 (5: 6: 6: 7: 7) sts at beg of next 2 rows. 66 (68: 68: 70: 72: 74) sts.
Dec 1 st at each end of next 3 rows, then on foll alt row, then on foll 4th row, then on 3 foll 6th rows. 50 (52: 52: 54: 56: 58) sts.
Work 3 rows.
Dec 1 st at each end of next and every foll alt row to 40 sts, then on foll 5 rows, ending with a WS row. 30 sts.
Cast off 3 sts at beg of next 2 rows.
Cast off rem 24 sts.

MAKING UP

Press all pieces with a warm iron over a damp cloth.
Join both shoulder and funnel neck seams using back stitch or mattress stitch if preferred.
Back opening edging
With RS facing and using 2.50mm (US C2) crochet hook, attach yarn at top of right back neck opening edge, 1 ch (does NOT count as st), 28 dc down right side of back opening, then 28 dc up left side of back opening, turn. 56 sts.

Next row (WS): 1 ch (does NOT count as st), 1 dc into each of first 33 dc, *2 ch, miss 1 dc (to make a button loop), 1 dc into each of next 3 dc, rep from * 4 times more, 2 ch, miss 1 dc (to make 6th button loop), 1 dc into each of last 2 dc.
Fasten off.
Join side seams. Join sleeve seams.
Insert sleeves. Sew on buttons.

Cardigan

BACK
Work as given for front of sweater to start of shoulder shaping, ending with a WS row.

Shape shoulders and back neck
Cast off 8 (8: 8: 9: 9: 10) sts at beg of next 2 rows.
66 (68: 70: 72: 74: 76) sts.
Next row (RS): Cast off 8 (8: 8: 9: 9: 10) sts, K until there are 12 (12: 13: 12: 13: 13) sts on right needle and turn, leaving rem sts on a holder.
Work each side of neck separately.
Cast off 4 sts at beg of next row.
Cast off rem 8 (8: 9: 8: 9: 9) sts.
With RS facing, rejoin yarn to rem sts, cast off centre 26 (28: 28: 30: 30: 30) sts, K to end.
Complete to match first side, reversing shapings.

Pattern note: Row-end edges of fronts forms actual front opening edges. To ensure edges remains neat and tidy, make sure new balls of yarn are joined in at side seam edges **only**.

LEFT FRONT
Cast on 180 (190: 200: 210: 220: 240) sts using 3¼mm (US 3) needles.
Row 1 (RS): *K2, lift 2nd st on right needle over first st and off right needle, rep from * to end. 90 (95: 100: 105: 110: 120) sts.
Row 2: K7, P to end.
Row 3: Knit.
These 2 rows set the sts - front opening edge 7 sts in g st with all other sts in st st.
Cont as set for a further 43 rows, ending with a WS row.
Row 47 (RS): K1 (1: 1: 1: 1: 0), (K2tog) 0 (0: 0: 0: 0: 3) times, *K2tog, K1, K2tog, rep from * to last 9 sts, K9.
58 (61: 64: 67: 70: 75) sts.
Keeping sts correct as set, work 13 rows.
Working all side seam increases as set by back, inc 1 st at beg of next and 3 foll 14th rows.
62 (65: 68: 71: 74: 79) sts.
Work 7 rows, ending with a WS row.

Shape front slope
Next row (RS): K to last 10 sts, K2tog tbl, K8.
61 (64: 67: 70: 73: 78) sts.
Working all front slope decreases as set by last row, dec 1 st at front slope edge on 4th and 4 (4: 5: 5: 5: 5) foll 4th rows **and at same time** inc 1 st at side seam edge of 6th row. 57 (60: 62: 65: 68: 73) sts.
Work 3 rows, ending with a WS row.

Shape armhole
Cast off 5 (5: 6: 6: 7: 7) sts at beg and dec 1 st at end of next row. 51 (54: 55: 58: 60: 65) sts.
Work 1 row.
Dec 1 st at armhole edge of next 5 (5: 7: 7: 9: 11) rows, then on foll 2 (4: 3: 4: 3: 4) alt rows, then on foll 4th row **and at same time** dec 1 st at front slope edge of 3rd and 2 (3: 3: 4: 4: 5) foll 4th rows. 40 (40: 40: 41: 42: 43) sts.
Dec 1 st at front slope edge **only** on 2nd (2nd: 2nd: 4th: 4th: 4th) and 6 (7: 4: 4: 2: 0) foll 4th rows, then on 2 (1: 3: 3: 5: 6) foll 6th rows.
31 (31: 32: 33: 34: 36) sts.
Cont straight until left front matches back to start of shoulder shaping, ending with a WS row.

Shape shoulder
Cast off 8 (8: 8: 9: 9: 10) sts at beg of next and foll alt row, then 8 (8: 9: 8: 9: 9) sts at beg of foll alt row. 7 sts.
Work in g st for a further 6.5 (7: 7: 7.5: 7.5: 7.5) cm on these sts only for back neck border extension, ending with a WS row.
Cast off.

RIGHT FRONT
Cast on 180 (190: 200: 210: 220: 240) sts using 3¼mm (US 3) needles.
Row 1 (RS): *K2, lift 2nd st on right needle over first st and off right needle, rep from * to end. 90 (95: 100: 105: 110: 120) sts.
Row 2: P to last 7 sts, K7.
Row 3: Knit.
These 2 rows set the sts - front opening edge 7 sts in g st with all other sts in st st.
Cont as set for a further 43 rows, ending with a WS row.
Row 47 (RS): K2, K2tog tbl, yfwd (to make a buttonhole), K5, *K2tog, K1, K2tog, rep from * to last 1 (1: 1: 1: 1: 6) sts, K1 (1: 1: 1: 1: 0), (K2tog) 0 (0: 0: 0: 0: 3) times.
58 (61: 64: 67: 70: 75) sts.
Working a further 5 buttonholes in this way on every foll 12th row and noting that no further reference will be made to buttonholes, cont as folls:
Keeping sts correct as set, work 13 rows.
Working all side seam increases as set by back, inc 1 st at end of next and 3 foll 14th rows.
62 (65: 68: 71: 74: 79) sts.
Work 7 rows, ending with a WS row.

Shape front slope
Next row (RS): K8, K2tog, K to end.
61 (64: 67: 70: 73: 78) sts.
Complete to match left front, reversing shapings.

SLEEVES (both alike)
Work as given for sleeves of sweater.

MAKING UP
Press all pieces with a warm iron over a damp cloth.
Join both shoulder seams using back stitch or mattress stitch if preferred. Join cast-off ends of back neck border extensions, then sew one edge to back neck. Join side seams. Join sleeve seams. Insert sleeves. Sew on buttons.

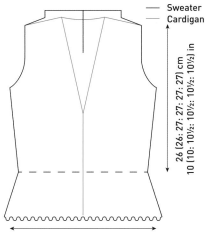

—— Sweater
—— Cardigan

26 (26: 27: 27: 27: 27) cm
10 (10: 10½: 10½: 10½: 10½) in

43 (45.5: 48: 50.5: 53: 57) cm
17 (18: 19: 20: 21: 22½) in

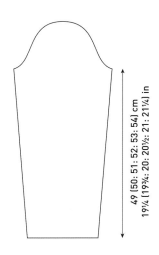

49 (50: 51: 52: 53: 54) cm
19¼ (19¾: 20: 20½: 21: 21¼) in

SCOUT
Belted jacket with cosy shawl collar

Recommendation
Suitable for the knitter with a little experience
Please see pages 30 & 31 for photographs.

	XS	S	M	L	XL	XXL	
To fit	**81**	**86**	**91**	**97**	**102**	**109**	**cm**
bust	32	34	36	38	40	43	in

Rowan Big Wool

	11	12	12	13	13	14x 100gm

Photographed in Prize

Needles
1 pair 9mm (no 00) (US 13) needles
1 pair 10mm (no 000) (US 15) needles

Tension
10 sts and 15 rows to 10 cm measured over
pattern using 10mm (US 15) needles.

Pattern note: The number of sts varies whilst
working patt. All st counts given presume there
are 8 sts in each patt panel (between markers/
asterisks) at all times.

BACK
Cast on 41 (43: 45: 49: 51: 55) sts using
10mm (US 15) needles.
Foundation row (WS): Knit.
Row 1 (RS): K6 (7: 8: 10: 11: 13), *place
marker on needle, yfwd, K8, yfwd, place marker
on needle*, K13, rep from * to * once more,
K6 (7: 8: 10: 11: 13).
Taking markers up work (by slipping marker
from left needle to right needle), cont as folls:
Row 2: K0 (0: 1: 0: 0: 2), P0 (1: 1: 0: 1: 1),
(K3, P1) 1 (1: 1: 2: 2: 2) times, K2, *K1, P8,
K1*, K2, (P1, K3) twice, P1, K2, rep from *
to * once more, K2, (P1, K3) 1 (1: 1: 2: 2: 2)
times, P0 (1: 1: 0: 1: 1), K0 (0: 1: 0: 0: 2).
Row 3: K6 (7: 8: 10: 11: 13), *K1, yfwd, K8,
yfwd, K1*, K13, rep from * to * once more,
K6 (7: 8: 10: 11: 13).
Row 4: K1 (2: 0: 1: 2: 0), P1 (1: 0: 1: 1: 1),
(K3, P1) 1 (1: 2: 2: 2: 3) times, *K2, P8, K2*,
(P1, K3) 3 times, P1, rep from * to * once
more, (P1, K3) 1 (1: 2: 2: 2: 3) times, P1
(1: 0: 1: 1: 1), K1 (2: 0: 1: 2: 0).
Row 5: K6 (7: 8: 10: 11: 13), *K2, yfwd, K8,
yfwd, K2*, K13, rep from * to * once more,
K6 (7: 8: 10: 11: 13).
Row 6: K0 (0: 1: 0: 0: 2), P0 (1: 1: 0: 1: 1),
(K3, P1) 1 (1: 1: 2: 2: 2) times, K2, *K1, P1, K1,
P8, K1, P1, K1*, K2, (P1, K3) twice, P1, K2, rep
from * to * once more, K2, (P1, K3) 1 (1: 1: 2:
2: 2) times, P0 (1: 1: 0: 1: 1), K0 (0: 1: 0: 0: 2).
Row 7: K6 (7: 8: 10: 11: 13), *K3, K4tog tbl,
K4tog, K3*, K13, rep from * to * once more,
K6 (7: 8: 10: 11: 13).
Row 8: K1 (2: 0: 1: 2: 0), P1 (1: 0: 1: 1: 1),
(K3, P1) 1 (1: 2: 2: 2: 3) times, *K8*, (P1, K3)
3 times, P1, rep from * to * once more, (P1,
K3) 1 (1: 2: 2: 2: 3) times, P1 (1: 0: 1: 1: 1),
K1 (2: 0: 1: 2: 0).
These 8 rows form patt.
Cont in patt, dec 1 st at each end of 5th and
3 foll 6th rows. 33 (35: 37: 41: 43: 47) sts.
Work 11 (11: 13: 13: 13: 13) rows, ending
with a WS row.
Inc 1 st at each end of next and 3 foll 6th rows,
taking inc sts into patt.
41 (43: 45: 49: 51: 55) sts.
Work 7 rows, ending after patt row 4 (4: 6:
6: 6: 6) and with a WS row. (Back should
measure 46 (46: 47: 47: 47: 47) cm.)

Shape armholes
Keeping patt correct, cast off 2 sts at beg
of next 2 rows. 37 (39: 41: 45: 47: 51) sts.
Dec 1 st at each end of next 1 (1: 1: 3: 3: 5)
rows, then on foll 1 (2: 2: 2: 2: 2) alt rows.
33 (33: 35: 35: 37: 37) sts.
Work 23 (21: 19: 17: 25: 23) rows, ending
after patt row 8 and with a WS row.
Now working sts between markers in st st
(instead of patt), cont as folls:
Work 0 (2: 4: 6: 0: 0) rows, ending with
a WS row. (Armhole should measures
19 (20: 20: 21: 22: 23) cm.)
Shape shoulders and back neck
Next row (RS): Cast off 5 sts, patt until there
are 5 (5: 6: 5: 6: 6) sts on right needle and
turn, leaving rem sts on a holder.
Work each side of neck separately.
Work 1 row. Cast off rem 5 (5: 6: 5: 6: 6) sts.
With RS facing, rejoin yarn to rem sts, cast off
centre 13 (13: 13: 15: 15: 15) sts, patt to end.
Complete to match first side, reversing shapings.

Pattern note: Row-end edges of fronts forms
actual front opening edges. To ensure edges
remains neat and tidy, make sure new balls
of yarn are joined in at side seam edges **only**.

LEFT FRONT
Cast on 30 (31: 32: 34: 35: 37) sts using
10mm (US 15) needles.
Foundation row (WS): Knit.
Row 1 (RS): K6 (7: 8: 10: 11: 13), place
marker on needle, yfwd, K8, yfwd, place marker
on needle, K16.
Taking markers up work (by slipping marker
from left needle to right needle), cont as folls:
Row 2: K5, (P1, K3) twice, P1, K2, *K1, P8,
K1*, K2, (P1, K3) 1 (1: 1: 2: 2: 2) times, P0 (1:
1: 0: 1: 1), K0 (0: 1: 0: 0: 2).
Row 3: K6 (7: 8: 10: 11: 13), *K1, yfwd, K8,
yfwd, K1*, K16.
Row 4: K7, (P1, K3) twice, P1, *K2, P8, K2*,
(P1, K3) 1 (1: 2: 2: 2: 3) times, P1 (1: 0: 1: 1:
1), K1 (2: 0: 1: 2: 0).
Row 5: K6 (7: 8: 10: 11: 13), *K2, yfwd, K8,
yfwd, K2*, K16.
Row 6: K5, (P1, K3) twice, P1, K2, *K1, P1, K1,
P8, K1, P1, K1*, K2, (P1, K3) 1 (1: 1: 2: 2: 2)
times, P0 (1: 1: 0: 1: 1), K0 (0: 1: 0: 0: 2).

Row 7: K6 (7: 8: 10: 11: 13), *K3, K4tog tbl, K4tog, K3*, K16.

Row 8: K7, (P1, K3) twice, P1, *K8*, (P1, K3) 1 (1: 2: 2: 2: 3) times, P1 (1: 0: 1: 1: 1), K1 (2: 0: 1: 2: 0).

These 8 rows form patt.

Cont in patt, dec 1 st at beg of 5th and 3 foll 6th rows. 26 (27: 28: 30: 31: 33) sts.

Work 11 (11: 13: 13: 13: 13) rows, ending with a WS row.

Inc 1 st at beg of next and foll 6th row, taking inc sts into patt and ending with a **RS** row. 28 (29: 30: 32: 33: 35) sts.

Shape for collar

Counting in from end of last row, place a 3rd marker after 5th st from end of row - this marker denotes front slope line. From this point on, all front opening edge /collar sts beyond this marker are worked in g st. Taking marker up work (by slipping arker from left needle to right needle), cont as folls:

Next row (WS): K3, inc in next st, K1, patt to end.

Work 1 row.

Next row: K3, inc in next st, K to front slope marker, patt to end.

Rep last 2 rows once more, ending with a WS row. 31 (32: 33: 35: 36: 38) sts.

Shape front slope

Next row (RS): Inc in first st (for side seam inc), K to within 2 sts of front slope marker, K2tog (for front slope dec), K to end.

Next row: K3, inc in next st (for collar inc), K to marker, patt to end. 32 (33: 34: 36: 37: 39) sts.

Working all front slope decreases and collar increases as set by last 2 rows, cont as folls: Inc 1 st for collar at beg of 2nd and foll 3 alt rows, then on foll 4th row, ending with a WS row, **and at same time** dec 1 st for front slope on 3rd and 2 foll 4th rows **and at same time** inc 1 st at beg (side seam edge) of 5th row. 35 (36: 37: 39: 40: 42) sts. (Left front should now match back to start of armhole shaping.)

Shape armhole

Keeping patt correct, cast off 2 sts at beg of next row. 33 (34: 35: 37: 38: 40) sts.

Work 1 row.

Dec 1 st at armhole edge of next 1 (1: 1: 3: 3: 5) rows, then on foll 1 (2: 2: 2: 2: 2) alt rows, ending with a RS row, **and at same time** dec 1 st for front slope on next and 0 (1: 1: 1: 1: 2) foll 4th rows **and at same time** inc 1 st for collar on 2nd and 0 (0: 0: 1: 1: 1) foll 4th row. 31 (30: 31: 32: 33: 32) sts.

Dec 1 st for front slope on 2nd (4th: 4th: 2nd: 2nd: 4th) and 5 (4: 4: 5: 5: 4) foll 4th rows

and at same time inc 1 st for collar on 3rd (next: next: 3rd: 3rd: next) and 4 (4: 4: 3: 3: 3) foll 4th rows. 30 (30: 31: 30: 31: 31) sts.

Work 1 (3: 3: 1: 3: 3) rows, ending with a WS row. (Left front should now match back to start of shoulder shaping.)

Shape shoulder

Keeping patt correct, cast off 5 sts at beg of next row, then 5 (5: 6: 5: 6: 6) sts at beg of foll alt row, ending at front opening/collar edge. 20 sts.

Shape collar

Row 1 (RS of collar, WS of body): K8, wrap next st (by slipping next st from left needle onto right needle, taking yarn to opposite side of work between needles and then slipping same st back onto left needle - when working back across wrapped sts work the wrapped st and the wrapping loop tog as one st) and turn.

Row 2 and every foll alt row: Knit.

Row 3: K14, wrap next st and turn.

Row 5: As row 3.

Row 7: As row 1.

Work 11 (11: 11: 13: 13: 13) rows, ending with a WS row. Cast off.

RIGHT FRONT

Cast on 30 (31: 32: 34: 35: 37) sts using 10mm (US 15) needles.

Foundation row (WS): Knit.

Row 1 (RS): K16, place marker on needle, yfwd, K8, yfwd, place marker on needle, K6 (7: 8: 10: 11: 13).

Taking markers up work (by slipping marker from left needle to right needle), cont as folls:

Row 2: K0 (0: 1: 0: 0: 2), P0 (1: 1: 0: 1: 1), (K3, P1) 1 (1: 1: 2: 2: 2) times, K2, *K1, P8, K1*, K2, P1, (K3, P1) twice, K5.

Row 3: K16, *K1, yfwd, K8, yfwd, K1*, K6 (7: 8: 10: 11: 13).

Row 4: K1 (2: 0: 1: 2: 0), P1 (1: 0: 1: 1: 1), (K3, P1) 1 (1: 2: 2: 2: 3) times, *K2, P8, K2*, P1, (K3, P1) twice, K7.

Row 5: K16, *K2, yfwd, K8, yfwd, K2*, K6 (7: 8: 10: 11: 13).

Row 6: K0 (0: 1: 0: 0: 2), P0 (1: 1: 0: 1: 1), (K3, P1) 1 (1: 2: 2: 2: 2) times, K2, *K1, P1, K1, P8, K1, P1, K1*, K2, P1, (K3, P1) twice, K5.

Row 7: K16, *K3, K4tog tbl, K4tog, K3*, K6 (7: 8: 10: 11: 13).

Row 8: K1 (2: 0: 1: 2: 0), P1 (1: 0: 1: 1: 1), (K3, P1) 1 (1: 2: 2: 2: 3) times, *K8*, P1, (K3, P1) twice, K7.

These 8 rows form patt.

Cont in patt, dec 1 st at end of 5th and 3 foll 6th rows. 26 (27: 28: 30: 31: 33) sts.

Work 11 (11: 13: 13: 13: 13) rows, ending with a WS row.

Inc 1 st at end of next and foll 6th row, taking inc sts into patt and ending with a **RS** row. 28 (29: 30: 32: 33: 35) sts.

Shape for collar

Counting in from beg of last row, place a 3rd marker after 5th st from beg of row - this marker denotes front slope line. From this point on, all front opening edge/collar sts beyond this marker are worked in g st. Taking marker up work (by slipping marker from left needle to right needle), cont as folls:

Next row (WS): Patt to last 5 sts, K1, inc in next st, K3.

Work 1 row.

Next row: Patt to front slope marker, K to last 4 sts, inc in next st, K3.

Rep last 2 rows once more, ending with a WS row. 31 (32: 33: 35: 36: 38) sts.

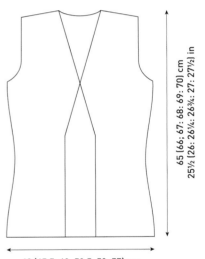

43 (45.5: 48: 50.5: 53: 57) cm
17 (18: 19: 20: 21: 22½) in

65 (66: 67: 68: 69: 70) cm
25½ (26: 26¼: 26¾: 27: 27½) in

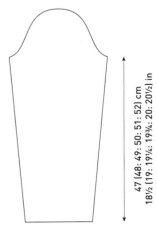

47 (48: 49: 50: 51: 52) cm
18½ (19: 19¼: 19¾: 20: 20½) in

Continued on next page...

BRACKEN

Long-line fringed scarf

Recommendation

Suitable for the novice knitter

Please see pages 48 & 49 for photographs.

Rowan Alpaca Chunky

5   x 100gm

Photographed in Dove

Needles

1 pair 10mm (no 000) (US 15) needles

Tension

9 sts and 14 rows to 10 cm measured over pattern using 10mm (US 15) needles.

Finished size

Completed scarf measures 20 cm (8 ins) wide and 290 cm (114 ins) long excluding fringe.

SCARF

Cast on 18 sts using 10mm (US 15) needles.

Row 1 (RS): K1, *yrn, P2tog, rep from * to last st, K1.

Row 2: As row 1.

These 2 rows form patt.

Cont in patt until scarf measures 290 cm (or length required), ending with a WS row.

Cast off.

Fringe

Cut 72 lengths of yarn, each 40 cm long, and knot groups of 4 of these lengths through cast-on and cast-off edges, positioning 9 knots evenly along each edge.

SCOUT – Continued from previous page.

Shape front slope

Next row (RS): K to front slope marker, K2tog (for front slope dec), patt to last st, inc in last st (for side seam inc).

Next row: Patt to marker, K to last 4 sts, inc in next st (for collar inc), K3. 32 (33: 34: 36: 37: 39) sts. Working all front slope decreases and collar increases as set by last 2 rows, complete to match left front, reversing shapings.

SLEEVES (both alike)

Cast on 23 (23: 25: 25: 27: 27) sts using 10mm (US 15) needles.

Foundation row (WS): Knit.

Row 1 & 3 (RS): Knit.

Row 2: K1 (1: 2: 2: 3: 3), *P1, K3, rep from * to last 2 (2: 3: 3: 0: 0) sts, P1 (1: 1: 1: 0: 0), K1 (1: 2: 2: 0: 0).

Row 4: K3 (3: 0: 0: 1: 1), *P1, K3, rep from * to last 0 (0: 1: 1: 2: 2) sts, P0 (0: 1: 1: 1: 1), K0 (0: 0: 0: 1: 1).

These 4 rows form patt.

Cont in patt, shaping sides by inc 1 st at each end of 9th and 1 (4: 2: 2: 1: 1) foll 14th (12th: 16th: 12th: 16th: 12th) rows, then on 2 (-: 1: 2: 2: 3) foll 16th (-: 18th: 14th: 18th: 14th) rows, taking inc sts into patt. 31 (33: 33: 35: 35: 37) sts. Cont straight until sleeve measures 47 (48: 49: 50: 51: 52) cm, ending with a WS row.

Shape top

Keeping patt correct, cast off 2 sts at beg of next 2 rows. 27 (29: 29: 31: 31: 33) sts. Dec 1 st at each end of next and 3 foll 4th rows, then on every foll alt row to 15 sts, then on foll row, ending with a WS row. Cast off rem 13 sts.

MAKING UP

Press all pieces with a warm iron over a damp cloth.

Join both shoulder seams using back stitch or mattress stitch if preferred. Join cast-off edges of collar sections, then sew row-end edge to back neck.

Join side seams. Join sleeve seams. Insert sleeves into armholes.

Belt

Cast on 7 sts using 9mm (US 13) needles. Work in g st until belt measures 140 (145: 150: 155: 160: 165) cm.

Cast off.

Try on jacket and mark position for belt. Make belt loops at this position over side seams (by making a short length of crochet chain).

WHITTLE
Ribbed fingerless mittens

Recommendation
Suitable for the knitter with a little experience
Please see pages 32 & 33 for photographs.

	XS	S	M	L	XL	XXL	
To fit	81	86	91	97	102	109	cm
bust	32	34	36	38	40	43	in

Rowan Lima
       2   x 50gm
Photographed in Argentina

Needles
1 pair 4½mm (no 7) (US 7) needles

Tension
22 sts and 31 rows to 10 cm measured over
stocking stitch using 4½mm (US 7) needles.

RIGHT HAND MITTEN
Cast on 58 sts using 4½mm (US 7) needles.
Row 1 (RS): P2, *K2, P2, rep from * to end.
Row 2: K2, *P2, K2, rep from * to end.
These 2 rows form rib.
Work in rib for a further 16 rows, ending with
a WS row.
Counting in from both ends of last row, place
markers after 17th st in from both ends of row
- 24 sts between markers.
Taking markers up work (by slipping marker
from left needle to right needle), cont as folls:
Row 19 (RS): Rib to first marker, slip marker
onto right needle, P2tog, rib to within 2 sts of
next marker, P2tog tbl, slip marker onto right
needle, rib to end.
56 sts.
Work 15 rows.
Row 35: As row 19. 54 sts.
Work 13 rows.
Row 49: As row 19. 52 sts.
Work 11 rows.
Row **61:** As row 19. 50 sts.
Work 11 rows.
Row 73: As row 19. 48 sts.
Work 9 rows, ending with a WS row.
Shape thumb opening
Next row (RS): Rib 39 sts and slip these sts
onto a holder, rib to end.
Work 9 rows on this set of 9 sts, ending with
a WS row.
Break yarn and leave these sts on another holder.

With **WS** facing, rejoin yarn to 39 sts left
on first holder and rib to end.
Work a further 8 rows on these 39 sts,
ending with a WS row.
Join sections
Next row (RS): Rib 39 sts on needle, then
rib across 9 sts on second holder. 48 sts.
Work a further 9 rows on all sts, ending with
a WS row.
Cast off in rib.
Join palm seam, preferably using mattress stitch.

LEFT HAND MITTEN
Work as given for right hand warmer to start
of thumb opening.
Shape thumb opening
Next row (RS): Rib 9 sts and slip these sts
onto a holder, rib to end.
Work 9 rows on this set of 39 sts, ending with
a WS row.
Break yarn and leave these sts on another holder.
With **WS** facing, rejoin yarn to 9 sts left on first
holder and rib to end.
Work a further 8 rows on these 9 sts, ending
with a WS row.
Join sections
Next row (RS): Rib 9 sts on needle, then rib
across 39 sts on second holder. 48 sts.
Work a further 9 rows on all sts, ending with
a WS row.
Cast off in rib.
Join palm seam, preferably using mattress stitch.

HEARTLAND
Chunky crochet jacket

Recommendation

Suitable for the crocheter with a little experience
Please see page 34 for photograph.

	XS	S	M	L	XL	XXL	
To fit	**81**	**86**	**91**	**97**	**102**	**109**	**cm**
bust	32	34	36	38	40	43	in

Rowan Alpaca Chunky

	10	11	11	12	13	14x100gm

Photographed in Pigeon

Crochet hooks

7.00mm (no 2) (US K10½) crochet hook
9.00mm (no 00) (US M13) crochet hook

Buttons - 4

Tension

9 sts and 7 rows to 10 cm measured over
pattern using 9.00mm (US M13) crochet hook.

Crochet abbreviations

ch = chain; **dc** = double crochet; **dc2tog** =
(insert hook as indicated, yoh and draw loop
through) twice, yoh and draw through all 3
loops; **ss** = slip stitch; **tr** = treble; **tr2tog** =
(yoh and insert hook as indicated, yoh and
draw loop through, yoh and draw through 2
loop) twice, yoh and draw through all 3 loop;
yoh = yarn over hook.

BACK

Make 40 (42: 44: 46: 48: 52) ch using
9.00mm (US M13) hook.
Foundation row (RS): 1 tr into 5th ch from
hook, 1 tr into ch **before** one just worked into
enclosing previous tr in this st, *miss next ch,
1 tr into next ch, 1 tr into missed ch enclosing
previous tr in this st, rep from * to last ch, 1 tr
into last ch, turn. 38 (40: 42: 44: 46: 50) sts.
Now work in patt as folls:
Row 1 (WS): 1 ch (does NOT count as st),
1 dc into each tr to end, working last dc into
top of 3 ch at beg of previous row, turn.
Row 2: 3 ch (counts as first tr), miss dc at
base of 3 ch, *miss next dc, 1 tr into next dc,
1 tr into missed dc enclosing previous tr in this
st, rep from * to last dc, 1 tr into last dc, turn.
These 2 rows form patt.
Work 3 rows.
Row 6 (RS): 3 ch (counts as first tr), 1 tr into
dc at base of 3 ch - 1 st increased, patt to last
dc, 2 tr into last dc - 1 st increased, turn.
40 (42: 44: 46: 48: 52) sts.
Work 1 row.
Row 8: 3 ch (counts as first tr), miss dc at
base of 3 ch, 1 tr into next dc, patt to last 2 dc,
1 tr into each of last 2 dc, turn.
Work 1 row.
Rep last 2 rows twice more.
Row 14 (RS): 3 ch (counts as first tr), miss dc
at base of 3 ch, 1 tr into next dc, 1 tr into
dc at base of 3 ch enclosing previous tr in this
st - 1 st increased, patt to last 2 dc, miss 1 dc,
1 tr into last dc, 1 tr into dc just missed
enclosing previous tr in this st, 1 tr into last dc -
1 st increased, turn. 42 (44: 46: 48: 50: 54) sts.
Work 5 (5: 5: 7: 7: 7) rows, ending with a
WS row. (Back should measure 29 (29: 29:
31: 31: 31) cm.)
Shape armholes
Next row (RS): Ss across and into 4th dc, 3 ch
(counts as first tr), miss dc at base of 3 ch, 1
tr into next dc - 3 sts decreased, patt to last 5
dc, 1 tr into each of next 2 dc and turn, leaving
rem 3 sts unworked - 3 sts decreased. 36 (38:
40: 42: 44: 48) sts.
Next row: 1 ch (does NOT count as st), dc2tog
over first 2 tr - 1 st decreased, 1 dc into each
st to last 2 sts, dc2tog over last 2 sts - 1 st
decreased, turn. 34 (36: 38: 40: 42: 46) sts.

Next row: 3 ch (counts as first tr), miss dc
at base of 3 ch, tr2tog over next 2 dc - 1 st
decreased, patt to last 3 dc, tr2tog over next
2 dc - 1 st decreased, 1 tr into last dc, turn.
32 (34: 36: 38: 40: 44) sts.
Next row: 1 ch (does NOT count as st), dc2tog
over first 2 tr - 1 st decreased, 1 dc into each
st to last 2 sts, dc2tog over last 2 sts - 1 st
decreased, turn. 30 (32: 34: 36: 38: 42) sts.
Rep last 2 rows 0 (0: 0: 1: 1: 1) times more.
30 (32: 34: 32: 34: 38) sts.
Work 7 (9: 9: 7: 9: 11) rows, ending with
a **RS** row.
Shape back neck
Next row (WS): Patt first 8 (9: 10: 8: 9: 11)
sts and turn, leaving rem sts unworked.
Next row: 3 ch (does NOT count as st), miss
dc at base of 3 ch - 1 st decreased, 1 tr into
next 1 (0: 1: 1: 0: 0) dc, patt to end, turn.
Work 1 row on these 7 (8: 9: 7: 8: 10) sts.
Fasten off.
Return to last complete row worked, miss next
14 (14: 14: 16: 16: 16) dc, attach yarn to next
st and cont as folls:
Next row (WS): 1 ch (does NOT count as st),
1 dc into st at base of 1 ch, 1 dc into each st
to end, turn. 8 (9: 10: 8: 9: 11) sts.
Next row: 3 ch (counts as first tr), miss dc
at base of 3 ch, patt next 4 (6: 6: 4: 6: 8) sts,
(1 tr into next dc) 1 (0: 1: 1: 0: 0) times,
tr2tog over last 2 dc - 1 st decreased, turn.
Work 1 row on these 7 (8: 9: 7: 8: 10) sts.
Fasten off.

POCKET LININGS (make 2)

Make 12 (12: 12: 14: 14: 14) ch using
9.00mm (US M13) hook.
Work foundation row as given for back.
10 (10: 10: 12: 12: 12) sts.
Beg with row 1, work in patt as given for back
for 4 rows, ending with a RS row.
Break yarn.

LEFT FRONT

Make 24 (26: 26: 28: 28: 30) ch using
9.00mm (US M13) hook.
Work foundation row as given for back.
22 (24: 24: 26: 26: 28) sts.
Now work in patt as given for back for 5 rows,
ending with a WS row.

Working all increases and decreases as given for back, cont as folls:
Inc 1 st at beg of next row, ending with a **RS** row. 23 (25: 25: 27: 27: 29) sts.

Place pocket

Next row (WS): Patt 8 sts, miss next 10 (10: 10: 12: 12: 12) sts and, in their place, patt across 10 (10: 10: 12: 12: 12) sts of first pocket lining, patt rem 5 (7: 7: 7: 7: 9) sts, turn.
Work 6 rows.
Inc 1 st at beg of next row. 24 (26: 26: 28: 28: 30) sts.
Work 5 (5: 5: 7: 7: 7) rows, ending with a WS row.

Shape armhole

Dec 3 sts at beg of next row.
21 (23: 23: 25: 25: 27) sts.
Dec 1 st at armhole edge of next 3 (3: 3: 5: 5: 5) rows. 18 (20: 20: 20: 20: 22) sts.
Cont straight until 5 rows less have been worked than on back to shoulder fasten-off, ending with a **RS** row.
Break yarn.

Shape neck

Next row (WS): Miss first 8 (9: 8: 10: 9: 9) sts, attach yarn to next st, 1 ch (does NOT count as st), 1 dc into st at base of 1 ch, patt to end, turn. 10 (11: 12: 10: 11: 13) sts.
Dec 1 st at neck edge of next 3 rows.
7 (8: 9: 7: 8: 10) sts.
Work 1 row more, ending with a WS row.
Fasten off.

RIGHT FRONT

Make 24 (26: 26: 28: 28: 30) ch using 9.00mm (US M13) hook.
Work foundation row as given for back.
22 (24: 24: 26: 26: 28) sts.
Now work in patt as given for back for 5 rows, ending with a WS row.
Working all increases and decreases as given for back, cont as folls:
Inc 1 st at end of next row, ending with a **RS** row. 23 (25: 25: 27: 27: 29) sts.

Place pocket

Next row (WS): Patt 5 (7: 7: 7: 7: 9) sts, miss next 10 (10: 10: 12: 12: 12) sts and, in their place, patt across 10 (10: 10: 12: 12: 12) sts of second pocket lining, patt rem 8 sts, turn.
Complete to match left front, reversing shapings and working first row of neck shaping as folls:

Shape neck

Next row (WS): Patt to last 8 (9: 8: 10: 9: 9) sts and turn, leaving rem sts unworked.
10 (11: 12: 10: 11: 13) sts.

SLEEVES (both alike)

Make 22 (24: 24: 24: 24: 26) ch using 9.00mm (US M13) hook.
Work foundation row as given for back.
20 (22: 22: 22: 22: 24) sts.
Now work in patt as given for back for 3 rows, ending with a WS row.
Working all increases as given for back, cont as folls:
Inc 1 st at each end of next and foll 6th row, then on 2 foll 8th rows.
28 (30: 30: 30: 30: 32) sts.
Work 1 (3: 3: 3: 5: 5) rows, ending with a WS row.

Shape top

Working all decreases as set by back armhole, dec 3 sts at each end of next row.
22 (24: 24: 24: 24: 26) sts.
Work 1 row.
Dec 1 st at each end of next 7 (8: 8: 8: 8: 9) rows, ending with a **RS** (WS: WS: WS: **RS: RS**) row. 8 sts.
Fasten off.

MAKING UP

Press all pieces with a warm iron over a damp cloth.
Join both shoulder seams using back stitch or mattress stitch if preferred. Join side seams.

Outer edging

With RS facing and using 7.00mm (US K10½) hook, attach yarn at base of left side seam, 1 ch (does NOT count as st), now work 1 round of dc across back hem edge, right front hem edge, up right front opening edge, around neck, down left front opening edge, then across left hem edge, working 3 dc into each corner point and ending with ss to first dc, do NOT turn.
Now work 1 round of crab st (dc worked from left to right instead of right to left) along these edges.
Fasten off.

Pocket edgings (both alike)

Work edging across both pocket opening edges in same way as given for outer edging.
Neatly sew pocket linings in place on inside.
Join sleeve seams. Sew sleeves into armholes.

Sleeve edgings (both alike)

Work edging across foundation ch edge of sleeves in same way as given for outer edging.
Sew buttons onto left front as in photograph, using "holes" of patt as buttonholes.

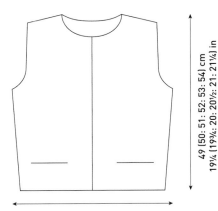

49 (50: 51: 52: 53: 54) cm
19¼ (19¾: 20: 20½: 21: 21¼) in

46.5 (49: 51: 53: 55.5: 60) cm
18 (19 : 20: 21: 22: 23½) in

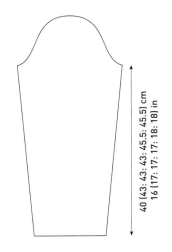

40 (43: 43: 43: 45.5: 45.5) cm
16 (17: 17: 17: 18: 18) in

HUNTER

Cropped cable & eyelet patterned sweater

Recommendation

Suitable for the knitter with a little experience
Please see page 39, 40 & 41 for photographs.

	XS	S	M	L	XL	XXL	
To fit	81	86	91	97	102	109	cm
bust	32	34	36	38	40	43	in

Rowan Big Wool

7 7 7 8 8 9 x 100gm
Photographed in Concrete

Needles

1 pair 8mm (no 0) (US 11) needles
1 pair 10mm (no 000) (US 15) needles
Cable needle

Tension

10 sts and 13 rows to 10 cm measured over
reverse stocking stitch using 10mm (US 15)
needles.

Special abbreviations

C6B = slip next 3 sts onto cn and leave at back
of work, K3, then K3 from cn;
C6F = slip next 3 sts onto cn and leave at front
of work, K3, then K3 from cn;
cn = cable needle;
MB = K into front, back and front again of next
st, turn, P3, turn, K3, lift 2nd and 3rd sts on
right needle over first st and off right needle.

Pattern note: When casting off sts, slip the
first st, rather than knitting it, so that the
shaped edge is a smoother edge without
jagged "steps".

BACK

Cast on 46 (48: 50: 54: 56: 60) sts using
8mm (US 11) needles.
Row 1 (RS): K0 (0: 0: 0: 0: 1), P0 (1: 2: 0: 1:
2), *K2, P2, rep from * to last 2 (3: 0: 2: 3: 1)
sts, K2 (2: 0: 2: 2: 1), P0 (1: 0: 0: 1: 0).
Row 2: P0 (0: 0: 0: 0: 1), K0 (1: 2: 0: 1: 2),
*P2, K2, rep from * to last 2 (3: 0: 2: 3: 1) sts,
P2 (2: 0: 2: 2: 1), K0 (1: 0: 0: 1: 0).
These 2 rows form rib.
Work in rib for a further 7 rows, ending with
a **RS** row.
Row 10 (WS): Rib 12 (13: 14: 16: 17: 19),
M1, rib 10, K2tog, rib 10, M1, rib 12 (13: 14:
16: 17: 19).
47 (49: 51: 55: 57: 61) sts.
Change to 10mm (US 15) needles.
Beg and ending rows as indicated and
repeating the 12 row patt rep throughout,
now work in patt from chart for body as folls:
Cont straight until back measures 32 (32: 33:
33: 33: 33) cm, ending with a WS row.

Shape armholes

Keeping patt correct, cast off 2 sts at beg of
next 2 rows.
43 (45: 47: 51: 53: 57) sts.
Dec 1 st at each end of next 3 (3: 3: 5: 5: 5)
rows, then on foll 1 (2: 2: 2: 2: 3) alt rows.
35 (35: 37: 37: 39: 41) sts.
Cont straight until armhole measures 18 (19:
19: 20: 21: 22) cm, ending with a WS row.

Shape shoulders and back neck

Next row (RS): Cast off 4 (4: 4: 4: 4: 5)
sts, patt until there are 8 (8: 9: 8: 9: 9)
sts on right needle and turn, leaving rem
sts on a holder.
Work each side of neck separately.
Cast off 4 sts at beg of next row (see pattern
note).
Cast off rem 4 (4: 5: 4: 5: 5) sts.
With RS facing, rejoin yarn to rem sts,
cast off centre 11 (11: 11: 13: 13: 13)
sts, patt to end.
Complete to match first side, reversing
shapings.

FRONT

Work as given for back until 8 rows less have
been worked than on back to start of shoulder
shaping, ending with a WS row.

Shape front neck

Next row (RS): Patt 13 (13: 14: 13: 14: 15)
sts and turn, leaving rem sts on a holder.
Work each side of neck separately.
Keeping patt correct, dec 1 st at neck edge
of next 4 rows, then on foll alt row.
8 (8: 9: 8: 9: 10) sts.
Work 1 row, ending with a WS row.

Shape shoulder

Cast off 4 (4: 4: 4: 4: 5) sts at beg of next row.
Work 1 row.
Cast off rem 4 (4: 5: 4: 5: 5) sts.
With RS facing, rejoin yarn to rem sts, cast off
centre 9 (9: 9: 11: 11: 11) sts, patt to end.
Complete to match first side, reversing
shapings.

SLEEVES (both alike)

Cast on 24 (24: 24: 26: 26: 26) sts using
8mm (US 11) needles.
Row 1 (RS): P1 (1: 1: 2: 2: 2), *K2, P2, rep
from * to last 3 (3: 3: 0: 0: 0) sts, (K2, P1) 1 (1:
1: 0: 0: 0) times.
Row 2: K1 (1: 1: 2: 2: 2), *P2, K2, rep from *
to last 3 (3: 3: 0: 0: 0) sts, (P2, K1) 1 (1: 1: 0:
0: 0) times.
These 2 rows form rib.
Work in rib for a further 8 rows, ending with
a WS row.
Change to 10mm (US 15) needles.
Beg and ending rows as indicated and
repeating the 12 row patt rep throughout,
now work in patt from chart for appropriate
sleeve as folls:
Inc 1 st at each end of 3rd and every foll
14th (14th: 16th: 16th: 16th: 12th) row to
28 (28: 32: 32: 32: 32) sts, then on every
foll 16th (16th: -: 18th: 18th: 14th) row until
there are 32 (32: -: 34: 34: 36) sts, taking
inc sts into st st.
Cont straight until sleeve measures 49 (50: 51:
52: 53: 54) cm, ending with a WS row.

Shape top

Keeping patt correct, cast off 2 sts at beg of
next 2 rows.
28 (28: 28: 30: 30: 32) sts.
Dec 1 st at each end of next and 3 foll 4th
rows, then on every foll alt row until 16 sts rem,
then on foll 3 rows, ending with a WS row.
Cast off rem 10 sts.

MAKING UP

Press all pieces with a warm iron over
a damp cloth.
Join right shoulder seam using back stitch
or mattress stitch if preferred.

Neckband

With RS facing and using 8mm (US 11)
needles, pick up and knit 10 sts down left side
of neck, 9 (9: 9: 11: 11: 11) sts from front, 10
sts up right side of neck, then 21 (21: 21: 23:
23: 23) sts from back.
50 (50: 50: 54: 54: 54) sts.
Row 1 (WS): P2, *K2, P2, rep from * to end.
Row 2: K2, *P2, K2, rep from * to end.
These 2 rows form rib.
Work in rib for a further 10 rows, ending with
a **RS** row.
Cast off in rib (on **WS**).
Join left shoulder and neckband seam.
Join side seams. Join sleeve seams.
Insert sleeves into armholes.

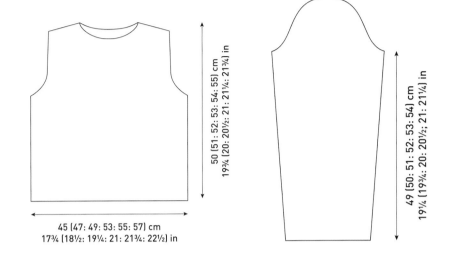

50 [51: 52: 53: 54: 55] cm
19¾ (20: 20½: 21: 21¼: 21¾) in

49 [50: 51: 52: 53: 54] cm
19¼ (19¾: 20: 20½: 21: 21¼) in

45 (47: 49: 53: 55: 57) cm
17¾ (18½: 19¼: 21: 21¾: 22½) in

Key

□	K on RS, P on WS
·	P on RS, K on WS
■	MB
⊙	yfwd on side (st st) panels, yrn on centre (rev st st) panel
⊠	K2 tog on side (st st) panels, P2tog tbl on centre (rev st st) panel
⊠	K2tog tbl on side (st st) panels, P2tog on centre (rev st st) panel

 C6B

C6F

Left sleeve chart

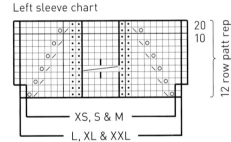

20
10

12 row patt rep

XS, S & M

L, XL & XXL

Right sleeve chart

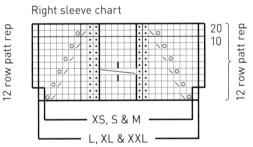

20
10

12 row patt rep

XS, S & M

L, XL & XXL

Body chart

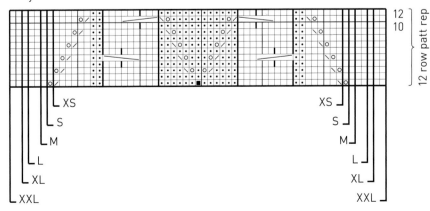

12
10

12 row patt rep

XS
S
M
L
XL
XXL

XS
S
M
L
XL
XXL

Recommendation
Suitable for the knitter with a little experience
Please see pages 36 & 37 for photographs.

	XS	S	M	L	XL	XXL	
To fit	81	86	91	97	102	109	cm
bust	32	34	36	38	40	43	in

Rowan Cashsoft 4 ply

| | 8 | 9 | 9 | 10 | 10 | 10 | x 50gm |

Photographed in Redwood

Needles
1 pair 2¼mm (no 13) (US 1) needles
1 pair 3mm (no 11) (US 2/3) needles

Buttons - 7

Tension
27 sts and 38 rows to 10 cm measured over
stocking stitch using 3mm (US 2/3) needles.

Special abbreviations
Tw2 = twist 2 as folls: K into front of 2nd st on
left needle, K first st, then slip both sts off left
needle together.

THORN
Cardigan with square neck & eyelet pattern

BACK
Cast on 225 (237: 249: 261: 273: 297) sts
using 2¼mm (US 1) needles.
Row 1 (RS): K3, *cast off 3 sts, K until there
are 3 sts on right needle after cast-off, rep from
* to end. 114 (120: 126: 132: 138: 150) sts.
Row 2: K to end, dec 1 st at end of row.
113 (119: 125: 131: 137: 149) sts.
Place markers at both ends of last row.
Cont in g st until work measures 4 cm from
markers, ending with a **RS** row.
Next row (WS): K12 (15: 18: 10: 13: 19), inc
in next st, *K10, inc in next st, rep from * to last
12 (15: 18: 10: 13: 19) sts, K12 (15: 18: 10:
13: 19). 122 (128: 134: 142: 148: 160) sts.
Change to 3mm (US 2/3) needles.
Following appropriate chart for size being
knitted, beg and ending rows as indicated and
rep the 20 row patt rep throughout, cont in
patt from chart for body as folls:
Dec 1 st at each end of 9th and 3 foll 8th rows.
114 (120: 126: 134: 140: 152) sts.
Work 7 rows, ending with a WS row.
Counting in from both ends of last row, place
markers on first (first: first: 2nd: 2nd: 2nd)
and 2nd (2nd: 2nd: 3rd: 3rd: 3rd) vertical
twist st ridges - 4 markers in total.
Row 41 (RS): P2tog, (patt to within 3 sts of
marked twist st ridge, yrn, P3tog, Tw2 - this
is marked twist st ridge, P2tog) twice, (patt to
within 3 sts of marked twist st ridge, P2tog,
Tw2 - this is marked twist st ridge, P3tog, yrn)
twice, patt to last 2 sts, P2tog.
104 (110: 116: 124: 130: 142) sts.
Noting that there is now one st less in rev st st
either side of marked twist st ridges, work 23
rows, ending with a WS row.
Row 65 (RS): Inc in first st, (patt to marked
twist st ridge, M1, Tw2 - this is marked twist st
ridge, M1) 4 times, patt to last st, inc in last st.
114 (120: 126: 134: 140: 152) sts.
Remove markers - rev st st panels either side
of marked twist st ridges now back to original
number of sts.
Cont in patt, inc 1 st at each end of 12th and
3 foll 12th rows, taking inc sts into rev st st.
122 (128: 134: 142: 148: 160) sts.
Cont straight until back measures 39 (39: 40:
40: 40: 40) cm from markers near cast-on
edge, ending with a WS row.

Shape armholes
Keeping patt correct, cast off 5 (5: 6: 6: 7: 7)
sts at beg of next 2 rows.
112 (118: 122: 130: 134: 146) sts.
Dec 1 st at each end of next 3 (3: 5: 5: 7: 9)
rows, then on foll 4 (6: 5: 7: 6: 8) alt rows,
then on 2 foll 4th rows.
94 (96: 98: 102: 104: 108) sts.
Cont straight until armhole measures 14.5
(15.5: 15.5: 16.5: 17.5: 18.5) cm, ending
with a WS row.
Now place g st section at back neck as folls:
Next row (RS): Patt 12 (13: 14: 16: 17: 19)
sts, (K10, K2tog) 5 times, K10, patt 12 (13: 14:
16: 17: 19) sts.
89 (91: 93: 97: 99: 103) sts.
Next row: Patt 12 (13: 14: 16: 17: 19) sts,
K65, patt 12 (13: 14: 16: 17: 19) sts.
This row sets the sts - centre 65 sts in g st with
edge sts still in patt.
Keeping sts correct as now set, work 11 rows,
ending with a **RS** row.
Shape back neck and shoulders
Next row (WS): Patt 12 (13: 14: 16: 17: 19)
sts, K10 and slip these 22 (23: 24: 26: 27: 29)
sts onto a holder, cast off next 45 sts knitwise
(one st on right needle), K9, patt 12 (13: 14:
16: 17: 19) sts.
Work each side of neck separately.
Cast off 7 (8: 8: 9: 9: 10) sts at beg of next
and foll alt row.
Work 1 row.
Cast off rem 8 (7: 8: 8: 9: 9) sts.
With RS facing, rejoin yarn to sts on holder
and patt to end.
Complete to match first side, reversing
shapings.

Pattern note: Row-end edges of fronts forms
actual front opening edges. To ensure edges
remains neat and tidy, make sure new balls
of yarn are joined in at side seam edges **only**.

LEFT FRONT
Cast on 135 (141: 147: 153: 159: 171) sts
using 2¼mm (US 1) needles.
Row 1 (RS): K3, *cast off 3 sts, K until
there are 3 sts on right needle after cast-off,
rep from * to end.
69 (72: 75: 78: 81: 87) sts.

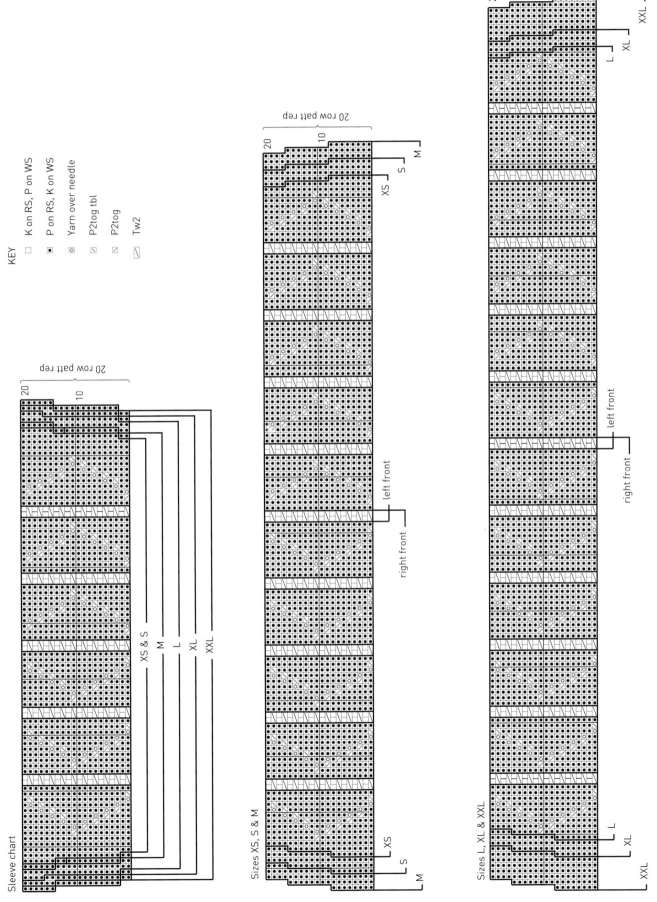

KEY

☐ K on RS, P on WS
⊡ P on RS, K on WS
⊙ Yarn over needle
⬦ P2tog tbl
⬦ P2tog
⬦ Tw2

Sleeve chart

20 row patt rep

XS & S
M
L
XL
XXL

Sizes XS, S & M

20 row patt rep

XS
S
M

left front

right front

Sizes L, XL & XXL

20 row patt rep

L
XL
XXL

left front

right front

Row 2: K38, K2tog, K to last 2 sts, K2tog. 67 (70: 73: 76: 79: 85) sts.

Place markers at both ends of last row.

Cont in g st until work measures 4 cm from markers, ending with a **RS** row.

Next row (WS): *K10, inc in next st, rep from * to last 12 (15: 18: 10: 13: 19) sts, K12 (15: 18: 10: 13: 19).

72 (75: 78: 82: 85: 91) sts.

Change to 3mm (US 2/3) needles.

Following appropriate chart for size being knitted and beg and ending rows as indicated, cont in patt from chart for body as folls:

Next row (RS): Work first 62 (65: 68: 72: 75: 81) sts as row 1 of chart, K10.

Next row: K10, work rem 62 (65: 68: 72: 75: 81) sts as row 2 of chart.

These 2 rows set the sts - front opening edge 10 sts in g st with rem sts in patt from chart. Keeping sts correct as now set, dec 1 st at beg of 7th and 3 foll 8th rows.

68 (71: 74: 78: 81: 87) sts.

Work 7 rows, ending with a WS row.

Counting in from end of last row, place markers on first (first: first: 2nd: 2nd: 2nd) and 2nd (2nd: 2nd: 3rd: 3rd: 3rd) vertical twist st ridges - 2 markers in total.

Row 41 (RS): P2tog, (patt to within 3 sts of marked twist st ridge, yrn, P3tog, Tw2 - this is marked twist st ridge, P2tog) twice, patt to end.

63 (66: 69: 73: 76: 82) sts.

Noting that there is now one st less in rev st st either side of marked twist st ridges, work 23 rows, ending with a WS row.

Row 65 (RS): Inc in first st, (patt to marked twist st ridge, M1, Tw2 - this is marked twist st ridge, M1) twice, patt to end.

68 (71: 74: 78: 81: 87) sts.

Remove markers - rev st st panels either side of marked twist st ridges now back to original number of sts.

Cont in patt, inc 1 st at beg of 12th and 3 foll 12th rows, taking inc sts into rev st st.

72 (75: 78: 82: 85: 91) sts.

Cont straight until left front matches back to start of armhole shaping, ending with a WS row.

Shape armhole

Keeping patt correct, cast off 5 (5: 6: 6: 7: 7) sts at beg of next row.

67 (70: 72: 76: 78: 84) sts.

Work 1 row.

Dec 1 st at armhole edge of next 3 (3: 5: 5: 7: 9) rows, then on foll 4 (6: 5: 7: 6: 8) alt rows, then on 2 foll 4th rows.

58 (59: 60: 62: 63: 65) sts.

Cont straight until 34 (34: 34: 38: 38: 38) rows less have been worked than on back to start of shoulder shaping, ending with a WS row.

Now place g st section at front neck as folls:

Next row (RS): Patt 12 (13: 14: 16: 17: 19) sts, (K10, K2tog) 3 times, K10.

55 (56: 57: 59: 60: 62) sts.

Next row: K43, patt 12 (13: 14: 16: 17: 19) sts. This row sets the sts - front opening edge 43 sts in g st with armhole edge sts still in patt. Keeping sts correct as now set, work 13 rows, ending with a **RS** row.

Shape front neck

Cast off 33 sts at beg of next row.

22 (23: 24: 26: 27: 29) sts.

Work 18 (18: 18: 22: 22: 22) rows, ending with a WS row.

Shape shoulder

Cast off 7 (8: 8: 9: 9: 10) sts at beg of next and foll alt row.

Work 1 row.

Cast off rem 8 (7: 8: 8: 9: 9) sts.

Mark positions for 7 buttons along left front opening edge - first to come level with 23rd row of patt (after g st border), last to come 10 rows below neck cast-off, and rem 5 buttons evenly spaced between.

RIGHT FRONT

Cast on 135 (141: 147: 153: 159: 171) sts using 2¼mm (US 1) needles.

Row 1 (RS): K3, *cast off 3 sts, K until there are 3 sts on right needle after cast-off, rep from * to end. 69 (72: 75: 78: 81: 87) sts.

Row 2: K2tog, K to last 40 sts, K2tog, K38. 67 (70: 73: 76: 79: 85) sts.

Place markers at both ends of last row.

Cont in g st until work measures 4 cm from markers, ending with a **RS** row.

Next row (WS): K12 (15: 18: 10: 13: 19), *inc in next st, K10, rep from * to end.

72 (75: 78: 82: 85: 91) sts.

Change to 3mm (US 2/3) needles.

Following appropriate chart for size being knitted and beg and ending rows as indicated, cont in patt from chart for body as folls:

Next row (RS): K10, work rem 62 (65: 68: 72: 75: 81) sts as row 1 of chart.

Next row: Work first 62 (65: 68: 72: 75: 81) sts as row 2 of chart, K10.

These 2 rows set the sts - front opening edge 10 sts in g st with rem sts in patt from chart. Keeping sts correct as now set, dec 1 st at end of 7th and foll 8th row.

70 (73: 76: 80: 83: 89) sts.

Work 5 rows, ending with a WS row.

Row 23 (RS): K4, cast off 2 sts (to make a buttonhole - cast on 2 sts over these cast-off sts on next row), patt to end.

Working a further 6 buttonholes in this way to correspond with positions marked for buttons and noting that no further reference will be made to buttonholes, cont as folls:

Dec 1 st at end of 2nd and foll 8th row.

68 (71: 74: 78: 81: 87) sts.

Work 7 rows, ending with a WS row.

Counting in from beg of last row, place markers on first (first: first: 2nd: 2nd: 2nd) and 2nd (2nd: 2nd: 3rd: 3rd: 3rd) vertical twist st ridges - 2 markers in total.

Row 41 (RS): (Patt to within 3 sts of marked twist st ridge, yrn, P3tog, Tw2 - this is marked twist st ridge, P2tog) twice, patt to last 2 sts, P2tog.

63 (66: 69: 73: 76: 82) sts.

Complete to match left front, reversing shapings.

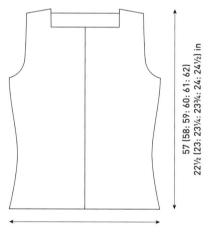

57 [58: 59: 60: 61: 62] cm
22½ [23: 23½: 23¾: 24: 24½] in

40.5 [43: 45.5: 48: 50.5: 54.5] cm
16 [17: 18: 19: 20: 21 ½] in

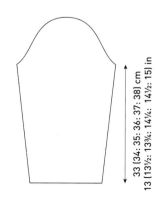

33 [34: 35: 36: 37: 38] cm
13 [13½: 13¾: 14¼: 14½: 15] in

Continued on next page...

HOMESPUN
Open work scarf

Recommendation
Suitable for the novice knitter
Please see page 12 for photograph.

Rowan Kidsilk Haze
        3   x 25gm
Photographed in Smoke

Needles
1 pair 4½mm (no 7) (US 7) needles
1 pair 9mm (no 00) (US 13) needles

Tension
12 sts and 19 rows to 10 cm measured over
pattern using a combination of 4½mm (US 7)
and 9mm (US 13) needles and yarn DOUBLE.

Finished size
Completed shawl measures 169 cm (66½ ins)
wide and is 69 cm (27 ins) deep.

SCARF
Cast on 1 st using 9mm (US 13) needles
and yarn DOUBLE.
Row 1 (RS): Using 4½mm (US 7) needle,
K into front and back of st. 2 sts.
Row 2: Using 9mm (US 13) needle,
inc in first st, K1. 3 sts.
Row 3: Using 4½mm (US 7) needle,
inc in first st, K1, inc in last st. 5 sts.
Row 4: Using 9mm (US 13) needle,
K2, P1, K2.
**Now using a 4½mm (US 7) needle
for all RS rows and a 9mm (US 13)
needle for all WS rows,** cont as folls:
Row 5: K2, yfwd, K1, yfwd, K2. 7 sts.
Row 6: K2, P3, K2.
Row 7: K2, yfwd, K to last 2 sts, yfwd, K2.
Row 8: K2, P to last 2 sts, K2.
Rows 9 and 10: As rows 7 and 8. 11 sts.
Row 11: K2, yfwd, K1, yfwd, K2tog, K1,
K2tog tbl, yfwd, K1, yfwd, K2. 13 sts.
Row 12: As row 8.
Row 13: K2, yfwd, K1, yfwd, K2tog,
K to last 5 sts, K2tog tbl, yfwd, K1,
yfwd, K2. 15 sts.

Row 14: K2, P to last 2 sts, K2.
Rows 15 to 44: As rows 13 and 14,
15 times.
45 sts.
Row 45: K2, yfwd, K1, yfwd, K to last 3 sts,
yfwd, K1, yfwd, K2. 49 sts.
Row 46: K2, P to last 2 sts, K2.
Row 47: K2, yfwd, K1, yfwd, K2tog,
K to last 5 sts, K2tog tbl, yfwd, K1, yfwd,
K2. 51 sts.
Row 48: As row 46.
Rows 49 to 76: As rows 45 to 48, 7 times.
93 sts.
Row 77: K2, yfwd, K1, yfwd, K to last 3 sts,
yfwd, K1, yfwd, K2.
97 sts.
Row 78: K2, P to last 2 sts, K2.
Rows 79 to 130: As rows 77 and 78,
26 times.
201 sts.
Row 131: K2, yfwd, K1, yfwd, K2tog,
K to last 5 sts, K2tog tbl, yfwd, K1,
yfwd, K2.
203 sts.
Cast off **very loosely** knitwise (on **WS**).

THORN – *Continued from previous page.*

SLEEVES (both alike)
Cast on 129 (129: 135: 141: 147: 153) sts
using 2¼mm (US 1) needles.
Row 1 (RS): K3, *cast off 3 sts, K until there
are 3 sts on right needle after cast-off, rep
from * to end. 66 (66: 69: 72: 75: 78) sts.
Row 2: K to end, inc (inc: -: inc: -: dec) 1 st
at end of row. 67 (67: 69: 73: 75: 77) sts.
Place markers at both ends of last row.
Cont in g st until work measures 4 cm from
markers, ending with a **RS** row.
Next row (WS): K0 (0: 1: 3: 4: 5), inc in next
st, *K10, inc in next st, rep from * to last 0 (0:
1: 3: 4: 5) sts, K0 (0: 1: 3: 4: 5).
74 (74: 76: 80: 82: 84) sts.
Change to 3mm (US 2/3) needles.

Beg and ending rows as indicated and rep
the 20 row patt rep throughout, cont in patt
from chart for sleeve as folls:
Inc 1 st at each end of 3rd and every foll
12th (10th: 12th: 14th: 12th: 12th) row
to 84 (78: 94: 94: 92: 90) sts, then on every
foll 14th (12th: -: 16th: 14th: 14th) row until
there are 90 (92: -: 96: 100: 102) sts, taking
inc sts into rev st st.
Cont straight until sleeve measures 33 (34:
35: 36: 37: 38) cm from markers, ending
with a WS row.
Shape top
Keeping patt correct, cast off 5 (5: 6: 6: 7: 7)
sts at beg of next 2 rows.
80 (82: 82: 84: 86: 88) sts.

Dec 1 st at each end of next 3 rows, then on
foll alt row, then on foll 4th row, then on 3 foll
6th rows. 64 (66: 66: 68: 70: 72) sts.
Work 3 rows.
Dec 1 st at each end of next and foll 4th row,
then on every foll alt row to 52 sts, then on foll
7 rows, ending with a WS row.
Cast off rem 38 sts.

MAKING UP
Press all pieces with a warm iron over a damp
cloth.
Join both shoulder seams using back stitch or
mattress stitch if preferred.
Join side seams. Join sleeve seams. Insert
sleeves into armholes. Sew on buttons.

MOONSTONE

Delicate cropped cardigan

Recommendation

Suitable for the knitter with a little experience
Please see page 44 for photograph.

	XS	S	M	L	XL	XXL	
To fit	**81**	**86**	**91**	**97**	**102**	**109**	cm
bust	32	34	36	38	40	43	in

Rowan Kidsilk Haze and Fine Lace

A Kidsilk Haze

	2	3	3	3	4	4	x 25gm

B Fine Lace

	1	2	2	2	2	3	x 50gm

Photographed in Kidsilk Haze in Pearl and Fine
Lace in Cameo

Needles

1 pair 3mm (no 11) (US 2/3) needles
1 pair 3¾mm (no 9) (US 5) needles

Buttons – 8

Tension

21 sts and 30 rows to 10 cm measured over
stocking stitch using 3¾mm (US 5) needles
and one strand each of yarns A and B held
together.

BACK

Cast on 68 (74: 80: 84: 90: 98) sts **loosely**
using 3mm (US 2/3) needles and one strand
each of yarns A and B held together.
Row 1 (RS): K0 (1: 0: 1: 0: 0), P0 (2: 1: 2: 1:
0), *K3, P2, rep from * to last 3 (1: 4: 1: 4: 3)
sts, K3 (1: 3: 1: 3: 3), P0 (0: 1: 0: 1: 0).
Row 2: P0 (1: 0: 1: 0: 0), K0 (2: 1: 2: 1: 0),
*P3, K2, rep from * to last 3 (1: 4: 1: 4: 3) sts,
P3 (1: 3: 1: 3: 3), K0 (0: 1: 0: 1: 0).
These 2 rows form rib.
Work in rib for a further 24 rows, inc 1 st at
each end of 13th of these rows and ending
with a WS row. 70 (76: 82: 86: 92: 100) sts.
Change to 3¾mm (US 5) needles.
Starting with a K row, now work in st st as folls:
Work 2 rows, ending with a WS row.
Next row (RS): K3, M1, K to last 3 sts, M1, K3.
Working all side seam increases as set by last
row, inc 1 st at each end of 8th and 3 foll 8th
rows. 80 (86: 92: 96: 102: 110) sts.
Cont straight until back measures 21 (21: 22:
22: 22: 22) cm, ending with a WS row.
Shape armholes
Cast off 4 (4: 5: 5: 6: 6) sts at beg of next
2 rows. 72 (78: 82: 86: 90: 98) sts.
Dec 1 st at each end of next 1 (3: 3: 5: 5: 7)
rows, then on foll 1 (1: 2: 1: 2: 2) alt rows, then
on foll 4th row. 66 (68: 70: 72: 74: 78) sts.
Cont straight until armhole measures 17 (18:
18: 19: 20: 21) cm, ending with a WS row.
Shape shoulders and back neck
Cast off 6 (6: 7: 7: 7: 8) sts at beg of next
2 rows. 54 (56: 56: 58: 60: 62) sts.
Next row (RS): Cast off 6 (6: 7: 7: 7: 8) sts,
K until there are 11 (11: 10: 10: 11: 11) sts
on right needle and turn, leaving rem sts
on a holder.
Work each side of neck separately.
Cast off 4 sts at beg of next row.
Cast off rem 7 (7: 6: 6: 7: 7) sts.
With RS facing, rejoin yarns to rem sts, cast off
centre 20 (22: 22: 24: 24: 24) sts, K to end.
Complete to match first side, reversing shapings.

Pattern note: Row-end edges of fronts forms
actual front opening edges. To ensure edges
remains neat and tidy, make sure new balls of
yarn are joined in at side seam edges **only**.

LEFT FRONT

Cast on 40 (43: 46: 48: 51: 55) sts **loosely**
using 3mm (US 2/3) needles and one strand
each of yarns A and B held together.
Row 1 (RS): K0 (1: 0: 1: 0: 0), P0 (2: 1: 2: 1:
0), *K3, P2, rep from * to last 5 sts, P5.
Row 2: K7, *P3, K2, rep from * to last 3 (1: 4:
1: 4: 3) sts, P3 (1: 3: 1: 3: 3), K0 (0: 1: 0: 1: 0).
Row 3: K0 (1: 0: 1: 0: 0), P0 (2: 1: 2: 1: 0),
*K3, P2, rep from * to last 5 sts, K5.
Row 4: P5, K2, *P3, K2, rep from * to last 3
(1: 4: 1: 4: 3) sts, P3 (1: 3: 1: 3: 3), K0 (0: 1:
0: 1: 0).
These 4 rows set the sts - front opening edge
5 sts in ridge patt and rem sts in rib as given
for back.
Cont as set for a further 22 rows, inc 1 st
at beg of 11th of these rows and ending
with a WS row. 41 (44: 47: 49: 52: 56) sts.
Change to 3¾mm (US 5) needles.
Row 27 (RS): K to last 5 sts, patt 5 sts.
Row 28: Patt 5 sts, P to end.
These 2 rows set the sts - front opening edge
5 sts still in ridge patt with all other sts now
in st st.
Keeping sts correct as now set and working
all side seam increases as set by back, inc
1 st at beg of next and 4 foll 8th rows.
46 (49: 52: 54: 57: 61) sts.
Cont straight until left front matches back to
start of armhole shaping, ending with a WS row.
Shape armhole
Keeping sts correct, cast off 4 (4: 5: 5: 6: 6) sts
at beg of next row. 42 (45: 47: 49: 51: 55) sts.
Work 1 row.
Dec 1 st at armhole edge of next 1 (3: 3: 5: 5:
7) rows, then on foll 1 (1: 2: 1: 2: 2) alt rows,
then on foll 4th row. 39 (40: 41: 42: 43: 45) sts.
Cont straight until 16 (16: 16: 18: 18: 18) rows
less have been worked than on back to start
of shoulder shaping, ending with a WS row.
Shape front neck
Next row (RS): K27 (27: 28: 29: 30: 32) and
turn, leaving rem 12 (13: 13: 13: 13: 13) sts
on a holder.
Dec 1 st at neck edge of next 4 rows, then
on foll 3 (3: 3: 4: 4: 4) alt rows, then on foll
4th row.
19 (19: 20: 20: 21: 23) sts.
Work 1 row, ending with a WS row.

Shape shoulder

Cast off 6 (6: 7: 7: 7: 8) sts at beg of next and foll alt row.

Work 1 row.

Cast off rem 7 (7: 6: 6: 7: 7) sts.

Mark positions for 8 buttons along left front opening edge - first, 2nd and 3rd buttons to come level with rows 3, 15 and 27, 8th button to come level with first row of neck shaping, and rem 4 buttons evenly spaced between.

RIGHT FRONT

Cast on 40 (43: 46: 48: 51: 55) sts **loosely** using 3mm (US 2/3) needles and one strand each of yarns A and B held together.

Row 1 (RS): P7, *K3, P2, rep from * to last 3 (1: 4: 1: 4: 3) sts, K3 (1: 3: 1: 3: 3), P0 (0: 1: 0: 1: 0).

Row 2: P0 (1: 0: 1: 0: 0), K0 (2: 1: 2: 1: 0), *P3, K2, rep from * to last 5 sts, K5.

Row 3: K1, K2tog tbl, yfwd (to make first buttonhole), K2, P2, *K3, P2, rep from * to last 3 (1: 4: 1: 4: 3) sts, K3 (1: 3: 1: 3: 3), P0 (0: 1: 0: 1: 0).

Row 2: P0 (1: 0: 1: 0: 0), K0 (2: 1: 2: 1: 0), *P3, K2, rep from * to last 5 sts, P5.

These 4 rows set the sts - front opening edge 5 sts in ridge patt and rem sts in rib as given for back.

Cont as set for a further 22 rows, making 2nd buttonhole as set by row 3 in row 15, inc 1 st at end of 11th of these rows and ending with a WS row.

41 (44: 47: 49: 52: 56) sts.

Change to 3¾mm (US 5) needles.

Row 27 (RS): Patt 1 st, work 2 tog tbl, yrn (to make 3rd buttonhole), patt 2 sts, K to end.

Row 28: P to last 5 sts, patt 5 sts.

These 2 rows set the sts - front opening edge 5 sts still in ridge patt with all other sts now in st st.

Making a further 4 buttonholes as set by row 27 and noting that no further reference will be made to buttonholes, keeping sts correct as now set and working all side seam increases as set by back, cont as folls:

Inc 1 st at end of next and 4 foll 8th rows.

46 (49: 52: 54: 57: 61) sts.

Complete to match left front, reversing shapings and working first row of neck shaping as folls:

Shape front neck

Next row (RS): Patt 1 st, work 2 tog tbl, yrn (to make 8th buttonhole), patt 2 sts, K7 (8: 8: 8: 8: 8) and slip these sts onto a holder, K to end.

27 (27: 28: 29: 30: 32) sts.

SLEEVES (both alike)

Cast on 59 (61: 63: 65: 69: 71) sts **loosely** using 3mm (US 2/3) needles and one strand each of yarns A and B held together.

Row 1 (RS): K1 (2: 0: 0: 1: 2), P2 (2: 0: 1: 2: 2), *K3, P2, rep from * to last 1 (2: 3: 4: 1: 2) sts, K1 (2: 3: 3: 1: 2), P0 (0: 0: 1: 0: 0).

Row 2: P1 (2: 0: 0: 1: 2), K2 (2: 0: 1: 2: 2), *P3, K2, rep from * to last 1 (2: 3: 4: 1: 2) sts, P1 (2: 3: 3: 1: 2), K0 (0: 0: 1: 0: 0w).

These 2 rows form rib.

Work in rib for a further 10 (12: 12: 14: 14: 16) rows, inc 1 st at each end of 5th of these rows and ending with a WS row.

61 (63: 65: 67: 71: 73) sts.

Change to 3¾mm (US 5) needles.

Shape top

Starting with a K row, now work in st st as folls:

Cast off 4 (4: 5: 5: 6: 6) sts at beg of next 2 rows.

53 (55: 55: 57: 59: 61) sts.

Dec 1 st at each end of next 3 rows, then on foll alt row, then on 5 foll 4th rows.

35 (37: 37: 39: 41: 43) sts.

Work 1 row.

Dec 1 st at each end of next and every foll alt row to 29 sts, then on foll 5 rows, ending with a WS row.

Cast off rem 19 sts.

MAKING UP

Press all pieces with a warm iron over a damp cloth.

Join both shoulder seams using back stitch or mattress stitch if preferred.

Neckband

With RS facing and using 3mm (US 2/3) needles, slip 12 (13: 13: 13: 13: 13) sts on right front holder onto right needle, rejoin yarns and pick up and knit 20 (20: 20: 22: 22: 22) sts up right side of neck, 28 (31: 31: 32: 32: 32) sts from back, and 20 (20: 20: 22: 22: 22) sts down left side of neck, then patt 12 (13: 13: 13: 13: 13) sts on left front holder.

92 (97: 97: 102: 102: 102) sts.

Row 1 (WS): Patt 5 sts, K2, *P3, K2, rep from * to last 5 sts, patt 5 sts.

Row 2: Patt 5 sts, P2, *K3, P2, rep from * to last 5 sts, patt 5 sts.

These 2 rows set the sts - 5 sts at each end of rows still in ridge patt with all other sts in rib.

Cont as set for a further 4 rows, ending with a RS row.

Cast off in patt (on **WS**).

Join side seams. Join sleeve seams.

Insert sleeves into armholes.

Sew on buttons.

38 (39: 40: 41: 42: 43) cm
15 (15¼: 15¾: 16: 16½: 17) in

38.5 (41: 43.5: 46: 48.5: 52.5) cm
15 (16:17: 18: 19: 20½) in

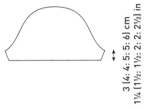

3 (4: 4: 5: 5: 6) cm
1¼ (1½: 1½: 2: 2: 2½) in

LEAF
Classic cardigan with shawl fronts

Recommendation
Suitable for the knitter with a little experience
Please see page 45 for photograph.

	XS	S	M	L	XL	XXL	
To fit	81	86	91	97	102	109	cm
bust	32	34	36	38	40	43	in

Rowan Baby Alpaca DK
| | 13 | 14 | 14 | 15 | 16 | 17 | x 50gm |
Photographed in Southdown

Needles
1 pair 3¼mm (no 10) (US 3) needles
1 pair 3¾mm (no 9) (US 5) needles

Tension
23 sts and 31 rows to 10 cm measured over
reverse stocking stitch using 3¾mm (US 5)
needles.

BACK
Cast on 105 (111: 117: 123: 129: 139) sts
using 3¼mm (US 3) needles.
Rows 1 to 4: Purl.
Change to 3¾mm (US 5) needles.
Starting with a P row, now work in rev st st
as folls:
Work 36 rows, ending with a WS row.
Next row (RS): P3, P2tog, P to last 5 sts,
P2tog tbl, P3.
Working all side seam decreases as set by
last row, dec 1 st at each end of 20th and
foll 20th row.
99 (105: 111: 117: 123: 133) sts.
Cont straight until back measures 45 (45: 46:
46: 46: 46) cm, ending with a WS row.
Shape armholes
Cast off 5 (5: 6: 6: 7: 7) sts at beg of next
2 rows. 89 (95: 99: 105: 109: 119) sts.
Dec 1 st at each end of next 3 (5: 5: 7: 7: 9)
rows, then on foll 3 (3: 4: 4: 5: 6) alt rows,
then on foll 4th row.
75 (77: 79: 81: 83: 87) sts.
Cont straight until armhole measures 18 (19:
19: 20: 21: 22) cm, ending with a WS row.
Shape shoulders and back neck
Cast off 7 (7: 8: 8: 8: 9) sts at beg of next
2 rows. 61 (63: 63: 65: 67: 69) sts.
Next row (RS): Cast off 7 (7: 8: 8: 8: 9) sts,
P until there are 12 (12: 11: 11: 12: 12) sts
on right needle and turn, leaving rem sts on
a holder.
Work each side of neck separately.
Cast off 4 sts at beg of next row.
Cast off rem 8 (8: 7: 7: 8: 8) sts.
With RS facing, rejoin yarn to rem sts, cast off
centre 23 (25: 25: 27: 27: 27) sts, P to end.
Complete to match first side, reversing
shapings.

Pattern note: Row-end edge of left front forms
actual front opening edge. To ensure edge
remains neat and tidy, make sure new balls
of yarn are joined in at side seam edge **only**.

LEFT FRONT
Cast on 82 (85: 88: 91: 94: 99) sts using
3¼mm (US 3) needles.
Rows 1 to 4: Purl.
Change to 3¾mm (US 5) needles.

Row 5 (RS): Purl.
Row 6: P6, K to end.
Last 2 rows set the sts - front opening edge
6 sts in purl g st and rem sts in rev st st.
Keeping sts correct as now set, work 34 rows,
ending with a WS row.
Working all side seam decreases as set
by back, dec 1 st at beg of next and 2 foll
20th rows.
79 (82: 85: 88: 91: 96) sts.
Cont straight until left front matches back to
beg of armhole shaping, ending with a WS row.
Shape armhole
Cast off 5 (5: 6: 6: 7: 7) sts at beg of next row.
74 (77: 79: 82: 84: 89) sts.
Work 1 row.
Dec 1 st at armhole edge of next 3 (5: 5: 7: 7:
9) rows, then on foll 3 (3: 4: 4: 5: 6) alt rows,
then on foll 4th row.
67 (68: 69: 70: 71: 73) sts.
Cont straight until left front matches back
to start of shoulder shaping, ending with
a WS row.
Shape shoulder
Cast off 7 (7: 8: 8: 8: 9) sts at beg of next and
foll alt row, then 8 (8: 7: 7: 8: 8) sts at beg of
foll alt row.
Work a further 21 (23: 23: 25: 25: 25) rows on
these 45 (46: 46: 47: 47: 47) sts only for back
neck border extension, ending with a WS row.
Cast off.

RIGHT FRONT
Cast on 82 (85: 88: 91: 94: 99) sts using
3¼mm (US 3) needles.
Rows 1 to 4: Purl.
Change to 3¾mm (US 5) needles.
Row 5 (RS): Purl.
Row 6: K to last 6 sts, P6.
Last 2 rows set the sts - front opening edge
6 sts in purl g st and rem sts in rev st st.
Complete to match left front, reversing
shapings.

SLEEVES (both alike)
Cast on 45 (47: 49: 51: 53: 55) sts using
3¾mm (US 5) needles.
Starting with a P row, now work in rev st st
as folls:
Work 14 rows, ending with a WS row.

Row 15 (RS): P3, M1, P to last 3 sts, M1, P3.
Working all increases as set by last row, inc 1
st at each end of 5 (3: 2: 0: 4: 2) foll 8th rows,
then on every foll 10th row until there are
71 (73: 75: 77: 81: 83) sts.
Cont straight until sleeve measures 45 (46: 47:
48: 49: 50) cm, ending with a WS row.

Shape top
Cast off 5 (5: 6: 6: 7: 7) sts at beg of next
2 rows.
61 (63: 63: 65: 67: 69) sts.
Dec 1 st at each end of next 3 rows,
then on foll alt row, then on 6 foll 4th rows.
41 (43: 43: 45: 47: 49) sts.
Work 1 row.
Dec 1 st at each end of next and every foll alt
row to 37 sts, then on foll 7 rows, ending with
a WS row.
Cast off rem 23 sts.

CUFFS (both alike)
Cast on 20 sts using 3¾mm (US 5) needles.
Row 1 (RS): Knit.
Row 2: K6, P to end.
These 2 rows set the sts - 6 sts in g st with
rem sts in st st.
Cont as set until row-end edge of cuff,
unstretched, fits neatly along cast-on edge
of sleeve, ending with a WS row.
Cast off.

MAKING UP
Press all pieces with a warm iron over
a damp cloth.
Join both shoulder seams using back stitch
or mattress stitch if preferred. Join cast-off
edges of back neck border extensions, then
sew row-end edge in place to back neck edge.
Join side seams. Join sleeve seams. Insert
sleeves into armholes. Join cast-on and cast-off
ends of cuff to form a loop. With RS of cuff
against WS of sleeve, sew st st row-end edge
of cuff to sleeve. Fold cuff to RS and secure
in place along sleeve seam.

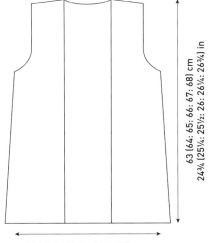

63 (64: 65: 66: 67: 68) cm
24¾ (25¼: 25½: 26: 26¼: 26¾) in

43 (45.5: 48: 50.5: 53: 57) cm
17 (18: 19: 20: 21: 22½) in

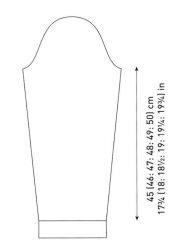

45 (46: 47: 48: 49: 50) cm
17¾ (18: 18½: 19: 19¼: 19¾) in

CRAFT
Pretty cabled sweater with back button fastening

Pattern note: To avoid cast-off edges stretching out of shape, dec sts whilst casting off as folls: across top of centre panel of back and front dec every 2 sts down to one st, at top of wide (8 st) cable dec the 8 sts down to 6 sts, and at top of narrow (4 st) cables dec the 4 sts down to 2 sts. All st counts given relate to the original number of sts and do **NOT** take into account these decreases.

BACK
Cast on 110 (116: 122: 126: 132: 140) sts using 3mm (US 2/3) needles and one strand each of yarns A and B held together.
Row 1 (RS): P2 (1: 0: 2: 1: 1), *K2, P2, rep from * to last 0 (3: 2: 0: 3: 3) sts, K0 (2: 2: 0: 2: 2), P0 (1: 0: 0: 1: 1).
Row 2: K2 (1: 0: 2: 1: 1), *P2, K2, rep from * to last 0 (3: 2: 0: 3: 3) sts, P0 (2: 2: 0: 2: 2), K0 (1: 0: 0: 1: 1).
These 2 rows form rib.
Work in rib for a further 9 rows, ending with a **RS** row.
Row 12 (WS): Rib 25 (28: 31: 33: 36: 40), (inc once in each of next 2 sts, rib 4) twice, inc once in each of next 2 sts, rib 5, inc once in each of next 22 sts, rib 5, inc once in each of next 2 sts, (rib 4, inc once in each of next 2 sts) twice, rib 25 (28: 31: 33: 36: 40).
144 (150: 156: 160: 166: 174) sts.
Change to 3¾mm (US 5) needles.
Beg and ending rows as indicated, working chart rows 1 and 2 **once only** and then repeating charts rows 3 to 34 **throughout**, cont in patt from chart for body as folls:
Cont straight until back measures 31 (31: 32: 32: 32: 32) cm, ending with a WS row.
Shape armholes
Keeping patt correct, cast off 6 (6: 7: 7: 8: 8) sts at beg of next 2 rows.
132 (138: 142: 146: 150: 158) sts.
Dec 1 st at each end of next 1 (3: 5: 5: 7: 7) rows, then on foll 8 (8: 7: 8: 7: 9) alt rows, then on foll 4th row.
112 (114: 116: 118: 120: 124) sts.**
Work 1 row, ending with a WS row.
Divide for back opening
Next row (RS): Patt 56 (57: 58: 59: 60: 62) sts, M1 and turn, leaving rem sts on a holder.
57 (58: 59: 60: 61: 63) sts

Work each side of neck separately.
Next row (WS): K1, patt to end.
Next row: Patt to last st, K1.
Last 2 rows set the sts - back opening edge st worked as a K st on every row with rem sts still in patt.
Cont as now set until armhole measures 18 (19: 19: 20: 21: 22) cm, ending with a WS row.
Shape shoulder and back neck
Keeping patt correct, cast off 9 (9: 9: 9: 10: 10) sts at beg of next row (see pattern note), 27 (28: 28: 29: 29: 30) sts at beg of foll row, 9 (9: 9: 9: 10: 10) sts at beg of next row, and 4 sts at beg of foll row.
Cast off rem 8 (8: 9: 9: 8: 9) sts.
With RS facing, rejoin yarns to rem sts, pick up and K one st from base of back opening, patt to end. 57 (58: 59: 60: 61: 63) sts.
Next row (WS): Patt to last st, K1.
Next row: K1, patt to end.
Last 2 rows set the sts - back opening edge st worked as a K st on every row with rem sts still in patt.
Complete to match first side, reversing shapings.

FRONT
Work as given for back to **.
Cont straight until 16 (16: 16: 18: 18: 18) rows less have been worked than on back to start of shoulder shaping, ending with a WS row.
Shape front neck
Next row (RS): Patt 36 (36: 37: 38: 39: 40) sts and turn, leaving rem sts on a holder.
Work each side of neck separately.
Keeping patt correct, dec 1 st at neck edge of next 6 rows, then on foll 3 (3: 3: 4: 4: 4) alt rows.
27 (27: 28: 28: 29: 30) sts.
Work 3 rows, ending with a WS row.
Shape shoulder
Cast off 9 (9: 9: 9: 10: 10) sts at beg of next and foll alt row **and at same time** dec 1 st at neck edge of next row.
Work 1 row.
Cast off rem 8 (8: 9: 9: 8: 9) sts.
With RS facing, rejoin yarns to rem sts, cast off centre 40 (42: 42: 42: 42: 44) sts, patt to end.
Complete to match first side, reversing shapings.

Recommendation
Suitable for the knitter with a little experience
Please see pages 51 to 54 for photographs.

	XS	S	M	L	XL	XXL	
To fit	**81**	**86**	**91**	**97**	**102**	**109**	cm
bust	32	34	36	38	40	43	in

Rowan Kidsilk Haze and Fine lace
A Kidsilk Haze
| | 6 | 6 | 6 | 7 | 7 | 7 | x 25gm |
B Fine Lace
| | 3 | 3 | 3 | 4 | 4 | 4 | x 50gm |
Photographed in Kidsilk Haze in Pearl and Fine Lace in Cameo

Needles
1 pair 3mm (no 11) (US 2/3) needles
1 pair 3¾mm (no 9) (US 5) needles
3.00mm (no 11) (US C2) crochet hook
Cable needle

Buttons - 2

Tension
Based on a stocking stitch tension of 21 sts and 32 rows to 10 cm using 3¾mm (US 5) needles and one strand each of yarns A and B held together.

Special abbreviations
C2B = slip next st onto cn and leave at back of work, K1, then K1 from cn; **C2F** = slip next st onto cn and leave at front of work, K1, then K1 from cn; **C4B** = slip next 2 sts onto cn and leave at back of work, K2, then K2 from cn; **C4F** = slip next 2 sts onto cn and leave at front of work, K2, then K2 from cn; **cn** = cable needle; **dc** = double crochet; **ch** = chain.

SLEEVE CHART

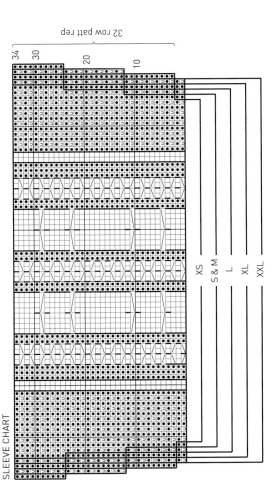

32 row patt rep

34 30 20 10

XS
S & M
L
XL
XXL

KEY

☐ K on RS, P on WS

● P on RS, K on WS

U K1 tbl

╲ C2B
╱ C2F
╲ C4B
╱ C4F

BODY CHART

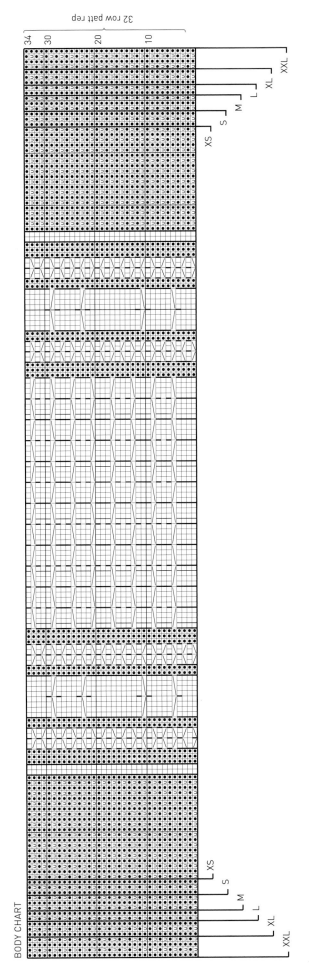

32 row patt rep

34 30 20 10

XS
S
M
L
XL
XXL

SLEEVES (both alike)

Cast on 56 (58: 58: 60: 62: 64) sts using 3mm (US 2/3) needles and one strand each of yarns A and B held together.

Row 1 (RS): K1 (0: 0: 0: 0: 1), P2 (0: 0: 1: 2: 2), *K2, P2, rep from * to last 1 (2: 2: 3: 0: 1) sts, K1 (2: 2: 2: 0: 1), P0 (0: 0: 1: 0: 0).

Row 2: P1 (0: 0: 0: 0: 1), K2 (0: 0: 1: 2: 2), *P2, K2, rep from * to last 1 (2: 2: 3: 0: 1) sts, P1 (2: 2: 2: 0: 1), K0 (0: 0: 1: 0: 0).

These 2 rows form rib.

Work in rib for a further 9 rows, ending with a RS row.

Row 12 (WS): Rib 15 (16: 16: 17: 18: 19), (inc once in each of next 2 sts, rib 4) 4 times, inc once in each of next 2 sts, rib 15 (16: 16: 17: 18: 19). 66 (68: 68: 70: 72: 74) sts.

Change to 3¾mm (US 5) needles.

Beg and ending rows as indicated and repeating the 32 row patt rep throughout, cont in patt from chart for sleeves as folls:

Inc 1 st at each end of 3rd and every foll 10th row to 72 (72: 80: 80: 90: 90) sts, then on every foll 12th row until there are 88 (90: 92: 94: 98: 100) sts, taking inc sts into patt.

Cont straight until sleeve measures 48 (49: 50: 51: 52: 53) cm, ending with a WS row.

Shape top

Keeping patt correct, cast off 6 (6: 7: 7: 8: 8) sts at beg of next 2 rows.

76 (78: 78: 80: 82: 84) sts.

Dec 1 st at each end of next 3 rows, then on foll 2 alt rows, then on 5 foll 4th rows.

56 (58: 58: 60: 62: 64) sts.

Work 1 row.

Dec 1 st at each end of next and every foll alt row until 48 sts rem, then on foll 7 rows, ending with a WS row.

Cast off rem 34 sts.

MAKING UP

Press all pieces with a warm iron over a damp cloth.

Join both shoulder seams using back stitch or mattress stitch if preferred.

Neckband

With RS facing, using 3mm (US 2/3) needles and one strand each of yarns A and B held together, starting and ending at back opening edges, pick up and knit 19 (20: 20: 21: 21: 21) from left back neck edge, 18 (18: 18: 19: 21: 21) sts down left side of neck, 20 (22: 22: 22: 22: 22) sts from front, 18 (18: 18: 19: 21: 21) sts up right side of neck, then 19 (20: 20: 21: 21: 21) from right back neck edge.

94 (98: 98: 102: 106: 106) sts.

Row 1 (WS): P2, *K2, P2, rep from * to end.

Row 2: K2, *P2, K2, rep from * to end.

These 2 rows form rib.

Work in rib for a further 8 rows, ending with a RS row.

Cast off in rib (on WS).

Back opening edging

With RS facing, using 3.00mm (US C2) crochet hook and one strand each of yarns A and B held together, attach yarn at top of neckband and work one row of dc evenly down first side of neck opening, then up other side of opening, turn.

Next row (WS): 1 ch (does NOT count as st), 1 dc into each dc down first side of opening then up other side of opening to neckband pick-up row, 6 ch (to make a button loop), 1 dc into each dc to last 2 dc, 6 ch (to make 2nd button loop), 1 dc into each of last 2 dc. Fasten off.

Join side seams. Join sleeve seams. Insert sleeves. Sew on buttons.

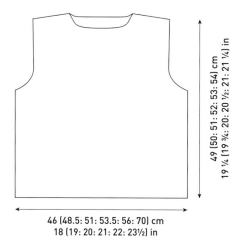

46 (48.5: 51: 53.5: 56: 70) cm
18 (19: 20: 21: 22: 23½) in

49 (50: 51: 52: 53: 54) cm
19 ¼ (19 ¾: 20: 20 ½: 21: 21 ¼) in

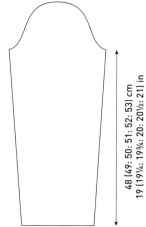

48 (49: 50: 51: 52: 53) cm
19 (19¼: 19¾: 20: 20½: 21) in

Recommendation

Suitable for the novice knitter
Please see pages 7 & 42 for photographs.

Rowan Alpaca Chunky or Big Wool

      2   x 100gm

Photographed in Alpaca Chunky in Pigeon, and
Big Wool in Smoky

Needles

1 pair 8mm (no 0) (US 11) needles
1 pair 10mm (no 000) (US 15) needles

Tension

Alpaca Chunky: 10 sts and 14 rows to
10 cm measured over reverse stocking
stitch using 10mm (US 15) needles.
Big Wool: 10 sts and 13 rows to 10 cm
measured over reverse stocking stitch
using 10mm (US 15) needles.

Pattern note: The pattern is written for
Alpaca Chunky, with the changes for Big Wool
indicated afterwards in brackets in bold.

TRANCE
Snug pull-on hat

HAT

Cast on 63 sts using 8mm (US 11) needles.
Row 1 (WS of hat, RS of turn-back): K1, *P1,
K1, rep from * to end.
Row 2: P1, *K1, P1, rep from * to end.
These 2 rows form rib.
Work in rib for a further 17 (**15**) rows,
ending with RS of hat facing for next row.
Next row (RS of hat, WS of turn-back): P2,
*P2tog, P1, P2tog tbl, P1, rep from * to last
st, P1.
43 sts.
Beg with a K row, work in rev st st for 6 rows,
ending with a **RS** row.
Place markers at both ends of last row.
Change to 10mm (US 15) needles.
Work in rev st st for a further 18 (**14**) rows,
ending with a **RS** row.
Shape top
Row 1 (WS): K1, (K2tog, K4) 7 times.
36 sts.
Work 1 row.
Row 3: K1, (K2tog, K3) 7 times. 29 sts.
Work 1 row.
Row 5: K1, (K2tog, K2) 7 times. 22 sts.
Work 1 row.
Row 7: K1, (K2tog, K1) 7 times.
15 sts.
Row 8: (P2tog) 7 times, P1.
Break yarn and thread through rem 8 sts.
Pull up tight and fasten off securely.
Join back seam, reversing seam below
markers for turn-back.

BANSHEE
Semi-fitted sweater with frill edged collar

Recommendation
Suitable for the knitter with a little experience
Please see pages 46 & 47 for photographs.

	XS	S	M	L	XL	XXL	
To fit	**81**	**86**	**91**	**97**	**102**	**109**	cm
hips	32	34	36	38	40	43	in

Rowan Kid Classic
7 8 8 9 9 10 x 50gm
Photographed in in Smoke

Needles
1 pair 3¾mm (no 9) (US 5) needles
1 pair 4mm (no 8) (US 6) needles
1 pair 4½mm (no 7) (US 7) needles

Tension
21 sts and 27 rows to 10 cm measured over
stocking stitch using 4½mm (US 7) needles.

BACK
Cast on 89 (95: 101: 105: 111: 119) sts
using 4mm (US 6) needles.
Row 1 (RS): K1 (0: 2: 0: 2: 1), P2 (1: 2: 1:
2: 2), *K3, P2, rep from * to last 1 (4: 2: 4:
2: 1) sts, K1 (3: 2: 3: 2: 1), P0 (1: 0: 1: 0: 0).
Row 2: P1 (0: 2: 0: 2: 1), K2 (1: 2: 1: 2: 2),
*P3, K2, rep from * to last 1 (4: 2: 4: 2: 1) sts,
P1 (3: 2: 3: 2: 1), K0 (1: 0: 1: 0: 0).
These 2 rows form rib.
Cont in rib, dec 1 st at each end of 13th and
foll 6th row. 85 (91: 97: 101: 107: 115) sts.
Work 3 rows, ending with a WS row.
Change to 4½mm (US 7) needles.
Beg with a K row, work in st st as folls:
Work 2 rows, ending with a WS row.
Next row (RS): K3, K2tog, K to last 5 sts,
K2tog tbl, K3.
Working all decreases as set by last row,
dec 1 st at each end of 6th and 2 foll 4th
rows. 77 (83: 89: 93: 99: 107) sts.
Work 13 rows, ending with a WS row.
Next row (RS): K3, M1, K to last 3 sts, M1, K3.
Work all increases as set by last row, inc 1 st
at each end of 8th and 4 foll 8th rows.
89 (95: 101: 105: 111: 119) sts.
Cont straight until back measures 38 (38: 39:
39: 39: 39) cm, ending with a WS row.
Shape armholes
Cast off 4 (4: 5: 5: 6: 7) sts at beg of next
2 rows. 81 (87: 91: 95: 99: 105) sts.
Dec 1 st at each end of next 3 (3: 5: 5: 7: 7)
rows, then on foll 2 (4: 3: 4: 3: 4) alt rows, then
on 2 foll 4th rows. 67 (69: 71: 73: 75: 79) sts.
Cont straight until armhole measures 18 (19:
19: 20: 21: 22) cm, ending with a WS row.
Shape shoulders and back neck
Cast off 5 (5: 5: 5: 6: 6) sts at beg of next
2 rows. 57 (59: 61: 63: 63: 67) sts.
Next row (RS): Cast off 5 (5: 5: 5: 6: 6) sts,
K until there are 9 (9: 10: 10: 9: 11) sts on
right needle and turn, leaving rem sts on
a holder.
Work each side of neck separately.
Cast off 4 sts at beg of next row.
Cast off rem 5 (5: 6: 6: 5: 7) sts.
With RS facing, rejoin yarn to rem sts, cast off
centre 29 (31: 31: 33: 33: 33) sts, K to end.
Complete to match first side, reversing
shapings.

FRONT
Work as given for back until 22 (22: 22:
24: 24: 24) rows less have been worked
than on back to start of shoulder shaping,
ending with a WS row.
Shape front neck
Next row (RS): K25 (25: 26: 27: 28: 30)
and turn, leaving rem sts on a holder.
Work each side of neck separately.
Dec 1 st at neck edge of next 6 rows,
then on foll 2 (2: 2: 3: 3: 3) alt rows,
then on 2 foll 4th rows.
15 (15: 16: 16: 17: 19) sts.
Work 3 rows, ending with a WS row.
Shape shoulder
Cast off 5 (5: 5: 5: 6: 6) sts at beg of next
and foll alt row.
Work 1 row.
Cast off rem 5 (5: 6: 6: 5: 7) sts.
With RS facing, rejoin yarn to rem sts, cast off
centre 17 (19: 19: 19: 19: 19) sts, K to end.
Complete to match first side, reversing
shapings.

SLEEVES (both alike)
Cast on 48 (48: 50: 52: 52: 54) sts using
4mm (US 6) needles.
Row 1 (RS): K0 (0: 0: 0: 0: 1), P0 (0: 1: 2: 2:
2), *K3, P2, rep from * to last 3 (3: 4: 0: 0: 1)
sts, K3 (3: 3: 0: 0: 1), P0 (0: 1: 0: 0: 0).
Row 2: P0 (0: 0: 0: 0: 1), K0 (0: 1: 2: 2: 2),
*P3, K2, rep from * to last 3 (3: 4: 0: 0: 1) sts,
P3 (3: 3: 0: 0: 1), K0 (0: 1: 0: 0: 0).
These 2 rows form rib.
Work in rib for a further 22 rows, inc 1 st at
each end of 13th of these rows and ending
with a WS row.
50 (50: 52: 54: 54: 56) sts.
Change to 4½mm (US 7) needles.
Beg with a K row and working all increases
in same way as back side seam increases,
now work in st st, shaping sides by inc
1 st at each end of 5th [3rd: 3rd: 3rd: next:
next] and every foll 14th (12th: 12th: 14th:
10th: 10th) row to 60 (58: 56: 70: 62: 72)
sts, then on every foll 16th (14th: 14th: -:
12th: 12th) row until there are 64 (66: 68:
-: 74: 78) sts.
Cont straight until sleeve measures 48 (49:
50: 51: 52: 53) cm, ending with a WS row.

Shape top

Cast off 4 (4: 5: 5: 6: 7) sts at beg of next
2 rows.
56 (58: 58: 60: 62: 64) sts.
Dec 1 st at each end of next 3 rows,
then on foll alt row, then on 5 foll 4th rows.
38 (40: 40: 42: 44: 46) sts.
Work 1 row.
Dec 1 st at each end of next and every foll
alt row until 34 sts rem, then on foll 5 rows,
ending with a WS row.
Cast off rem 24 sts.

MAKING UP

Press all pieces with a warm iron over
a damp cloth.
Join right shoulder seam using back stitch
or mattress stitch if preferred.

Collar

With RS facing and using 3¾mm (US 5)
needles, pick up and knit 27 (27: 27: 29: 29:
29) sts down left side of neck, 17 (19: 19: 19:
19: 19) sts from front, 27 (27: 27: 29: 29: 29)
sts up right side of neck, then 38 (40: 40: 42:
42: 42) sts from back.
109 (113: 113: 119: 119: 119) sts.
Beg with a K row, work in st st for 10 cm,
ending with a P row.
Change to 4½mm (US 7) needles.
Cont in st st until collar measures 25 cm
from pick-up row, ending with a P row.
Change to 3¾mm (US 5) needles.
Next row (RS of collar, WS of body): Knit.
Next row: Purl.
Next row: Inc once knitwise in each st to last
st, K1.
217 (225: 225: 237: 237: 237) sts.
Next row: Inc once purlwise in each st to last
st, P1.
433 (449: 449: 473: 473: 473) sts.
Cast off.
Join left shoulder and collar seam, reversing
seam for collar. Join side seams.
Join sleeve seams.
Insert sleeves into armholes.

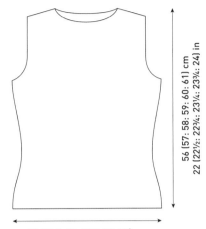

43 (45.5: 48: 50.5: 53: 57) cm
17 (18: 19: 20: 21: 22½) in

56 (57: 58: 59: 60: 61) cm
22 (22½: 22¾: 23¼: 23¾: 24) in

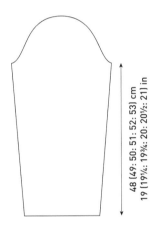

48 (49: 50: 51: 52: 53) cm
19 (19¼: 19¾: 20: 20½: 21) in

INFORMATION

A guide to assist with techniques & finishing touches

TENSION

Achieving the correct tension has to be one of the most important elements in producing a beautiful, well fitting knitted garment.

The tension controls the size and shape of your finished piece and any variation to either stitches or rows, however slight, will affect your work and change the fit completely.

To avoid any disappointment, we would always recommend that you knit a tension square in the yarn and stitch given in the pattern, working perhaps four or five more stitches and rows than those given in the tension note.

When counting the tension, place your knitting on a flat surface and mark out a 10cm square with pins. Count the stitches between the pins. If you have too many stitches to 10cm your knitting it too tight, try again using thicker needles, if you have too few stitches to 10cm your knitting is too loose, so try again using finer needles. Please note, if you are unable to achieve the correct stitches and rows required, the stitches are more crucial as many patterns are knitted to length. Keep an eye on your tension during knitting, especially if you're going back to work which has been put to one side for any length of time.

SIZING

The instructions are given for the smallest size. Where they vary, work the figures in brackets for the larger sizes. One set of figures refers to all sizes. The size diagram with each pattern will help you decide which size to knit. The measurements given on the size diagram are the actual size your garment should be when completed.

Measurements will vary from design to design because the necessary ease allowances have been made in each pattern to give your garment the correct fit, i.e. a loose fitting garment will be several cm wider than a neat fitted one, a snug fitting garment may have no ease at all.

CHART NOTE

Some of our patterns include a chart. Each square on a chart represent a stitch and each line of squares a row of knitting.

When working from a chart, unless otherwise stated, read odd rows (RS) from right to left and even rows (WS) from left to right. The key alongside each chart indicates how each stitch is worked.

FINISHING INSTRUCTIONS

It is the pressing and finishing which will transform your knitted pieces into a garment to be proud of.

Pressing

Darn in ends neatly along the selvage edge. Follow closely any special instructions given on the pattern or ball band and always take great care not to over press your work. Block out your knitting on a pressing or ironing board, easing into shape, and unless otherwise states, press each piece using a warm iron over a damp cloth.

Tip: Attention should be given to ribs/edgings; if the garment is close fitting – steam the ribs gently so that the stitches fill out but stay elastic. Alternatively if the garment is to hang straight then steam out to the correct shape.

Tip: Take special care to press the selvages, as this will make sewing up both easier and neater.

CONSTRUCTION
Stitching together

When stitching the pieces together, remember to match areas of pattern very carefully where they meet.

Use a stitch such as back stitch or mattress stitch for all main knitting seams and join all ribs and neckband with mattress stitch, unless otherwise stated.

Take extra care when stitching the edgings and collars around the back neck of a garment.

They control the width of the back neck, and if too wide the garment will be ill fitting and drop off the shoulder. Knit back neck edgings only to the length stated in the pattern, even stretching it slightly if for example, you are working in garter or horizontal rib stitch. Stitch edgings/collars firmly into place using a back stitch seam, easing-in the back neck to fit the collar/edging rather than stretching the collar/edging to fit the back neck.

Set-in sleeves: Join side and sleeve seams. Place centre of cast off edge of sleeve to shoulder seams. Set in sleeve, easing sleeve head into armhole.

Square set in sleeves: Set the sleeve top into armhole, the straight sides at top of sleeve to form a neat right-angle to cast off stitches at armhole on back and front.

CARE INSTRUCTIONS
Yarns

Follow the care instructions printed on each individual ball band. Where different yarns are used in the same garment, follow the care instructions for the more delicate one.

Buttons

We recommend that buttons are removed if your garment is to be machine washed.

CROCHET

We are aware that crochet terminology varies from country to country. Please note we have used the English style in this publication.

Crochet abbreviations

ch	chain
ss	slip stitch
dc	double crochet
htr	half treble
tr	treble
dtr	double treble
htr2tog	half treble 2tog
tr2tog	treble 2tog
yoh	yarn over hook
sp(s)	space(s)

Double crochet

1 Insert the hook into the work (as indicated in the pattern), wrap the yarn over the hook and draw the yarn through the work only.
2 Wrap the yarn again and draw the yarn through both loops on the hook.
3 1 dc made

Half treble

1 Wrap the yarn over the hook & insert the hook into the work (as indicated in pattern).
2 Wrap the yarn over the hook draw through the work only and wrap the yarn again.
3 Draw through all 3 loops on the hook.
4 1 half treble made.

Treble

1 Wrap the yarn over the hook and insert the hook into the work (as indicated on the pattern).
2 Wrap the yarn over the hook draw through the work only and wrap the yarn again.
3 Draw through the first 2 loops only and wrap the yarn again.
4 Draw through the last 2 loops on the hook.
5 1 treble made.

ABBREVIATIONS

K	knit
P	purl
K1b	knit 1 through back loop
st(s)	stitch(es)
inc	increase(e)(ing)
dec	decrease(e)(ing)
st st	stocking stitch (1 row K, 1 row P)
garter st	garter stitch (K every row)
beg	begin(ning)
foll	following
rem	remain(ing)
rev st st	reverse stocking stitch (1 row P, 1 row K)
rep	repeat
alt	alternate
cont	continue
patt	pattern
tog	together
mm	millimetres
cm	centimetres
in(s)	inch(es)
RS	right side
WS	wrong side
sl 1	slip one stitch
psso	pass slipped stitch over
tbl	through back of loop
M1	make one stitch by picking up horizontal loop before next stitch and knitting into back of it
M1p	make one stitch by picking up horizontal loop before next stitch and purling into back of it
yfwd	yarn forward
yon	yarn over needle
yrn	yarn round needle
MP	Make picot: Cast on 1 st, by inserting the right needle between the first and second stitch on left needle, take yarn round needle, bring loop through and place on left (one stitch cast on), cast off 1 st, by knitting first the loop and then the next stitch, pass the first stitch over the second (one stitch cast off).
Cn	cable needle
C4B	Cable 4 back: Slip next 2 sts onto a cn and hold at back of work, K2, K2 from cn.
C4F	Cable 4 front: Slip next 2 sts onto a cn and hold at front of work, K2, K2 from cn.